Nancy,
The se
ending. · your own · J t is worth the effort.
Love
Morris T. Johnston

GOD IS

by
MORRIS T. JOHNSTONE

PUBLISHING

Note for Librarians: A cataloguing record for this book is available from Library
and Archives Canada at www.collectionscanada.ca/amicus/index-c.html

ISBN 1-4120-8801-1

Printed in Victoria, BC, Canada. Printed on paper with minimum 30% recycled fibre.
Trafford's print shop runs on "green energy" from solar, wind and other environmentally-friendly
power sources.

Offices in Canada, USA, Ireland and UK

Book sales for North America and international:
Trafford Publishing, 6E–2333 Government St.,
Victoria, BC V8T 4P4 CANADA
phone 250 383 6864 (toll-free 1 888 232 4444)
fax 250 383 6804; email to orders@trafford.com
Book sales in Europe:
Trafford Publishing (UK) Limited, 9 Park End Street, 2nd Floor
Oxford, UK OX1 1HH UNITED KINGDOM
phone 44 (0)1865 722 113 (local rate 0845 230 9601)
facsimile 44 (0)1865 722 868; info.uk@trafford.com
Order online at:
trafford.com/06-0557

10 9 8 7 6 5 4 3

This book is dedicated to my wife
Doris, whose patience with my
time, cloistered in the study
left her wondering what I was
up to, and to my late father
Thomas A. Johnstone who taught
me to seek understanding.
I have been influenced by some
of the great thinkers of modern
times.   However the work and
thoughts are mine.

Cover by:
Lazercolor Media Group
Lloydminster Alberta.

God Is

Preface

The information in this book is the best I can do to make sense of our world. Our world is not an accident. There is an intelligent power directing our progress to the extent that we allow or co-operate with "IT."

While it is possible to mount an opposite position on any one of these premises, it seems that one must set some landmarks by which to determine ones direction in life. If time indicates a need to re-evaluate and update, so be it. Those in "the know" a few hundred years ago "knew" that the earth was flat. Can we allow similar traditions to continue to imprison us today?

Each chapter is closed with an affirmative prayer. These prayers are written in the first person so that the reader can take them personally. They affirm the truth and the faith expressed in that chapter. One writer has said that "all things are a compound in one." This work is my attempt to express the connectedness of all things. To me the interdependence of life forms, and the way that nature is balanced seem to support this affirmation. If our existence is not an accident then there must be a purpose in our creation. Our movement from the caves to the modern world suggests that such purpose might be to find joy in our lives. Our penchant for fear, war, and hate make the possibility of joy a goal that we can only attain when we choose a more intelligent way.

Because the Bible has much good information and because it has status with many people, I will use selected quotes from it. (Mostly King James or New Century versions.)

In these pages I believe a more intelligent way is outlined. However, it is not a new way.

It is a way that was outlined thousands of years ago. It has been delivered by prophets and sages in all cultures. However, people have twisted and reformed and applied their own wisdom in tinkering with it till the original version is totally unrecognizable. The basic message is that God is LOVE and supports life. God does not take sides and God does not have temper tantrums. Such concepts are evidence of human tampering and distortion of the message. In some circles it would be called "apostasy" or "falling away" from the original information. It is my hope that the reader may find some light and hope in these pages. They are the result of 75 years of study, questioning and observation by the writer. However they may seem to the reader, they are not by any means the final answer to the challenge of living. Morris

One: Who Or What is God?

"God does exist." Or "God does not exist." How can I prove either one of these assertions? In either case what I have is only a faith statement. There is no way that I know of to prove either one. If God does exist, what kind of God is it? Is it personal or aloof? Is It local or non-local? This is part of the "mystery" of God.

Once I have chosen to commit to "God is" or "God is not" I can begin to collect evidence to support my assertion. I choose to believe that "nothing comes from nothing." This is an old adage but my life experience supports the concept. Therefore something moved to trigger the "big Bang," if you insist on such an event. The reality is that the big bang is a faith statement also. I see this as only a small bang. A bang that has been repeated many times over in the endless reaches of time.   I Am told that Black Holes implode only to "bang" outward again when the pressures get too great. That is how I see the bang.

The universe is self sustaining because all is recycled and all things cycle from water to carbon to the galaxies themselves. A pretty ingenious system and one that, to my mind requires a very intelligent instigator. (The only trouble with this system, as far as we are concerned, is the varying

3

length of the cycle. Carbon that took millions of years to store in the form of coal and oil is being released in a few hundred years and this may cause a disaster for us. Of course this is not the systems fault it is ours.) My faith statement is that God is that instigator or founder of the universe: a pretty intelligent system. I believe that "The glory of God Is intelligence." Another name for God might be "The Universe" or even "life."(I would also expect that an intelligent God; or the Universe would have intelligent residents and expect them to be intelligent in their processes. We will attempt to point out where God is later in this work.)

As the source and power behind all things it is essential for me to   believe in God.

We say that God is the "Uncreated One" and then proceed to "create" (imagine) God in our own image. This is the anthropomorphic god. The god formed in man' image. Thinking people very often, recognizing this, decide that the whole thing is a myth and reject the whole concept of God out of hand.   However, chance is a poor substitute for God. Sure the universe "just happened."

 This is fine, except that I see order within the chaos of the universe. If I showed my new car to a friend and he asked "who made it" to which I replied "no-one, it just happened." Would my friend not be sure that I was candidate number one for the loony bin? Now the car is a complex unit made up of many opposing parts. Note that the opposing parts work together to produce a satisfactory performance in the car. These parts are organized in a precise manner. It is a reflection of a high level of intelligence. The universe which runs so well, that we can set our watches by the sun. The earth where everything re-cycles so that it is virtually self-sustaining reflects to me a higher degree of intelligent thought. The car certainly is not smart enough to recycle itself. The thought and planning required to set up the universe require of me that I recognize a maker.

Concepts of God have evolved over the centuries. The "tribal god" of ancient Israel reported in the Old Testament does not meet the requirements of a world now known to be comprised of galaxies. Remember that the Israelites thought the world was flat and had a lid on it that God opened when it rained. 1 (The word "firmament is from the Latin for support. The sky was thought to be the lid and God opened the windows to allow the flood.) This tribal god also had a temper and drowned or rained fire on those with whom he was displeased. Just like some petty dictators of our own day. This same kind of thinking was scoffed at by the white explorers when found among the natives of Oceania and some primitives in far places.

Remember that some of these folks offered a virgin to the volcano in an effort to quiet it. In this kind of the thinking landslides, tsunamis and other natural disasters are seen as judgments of an angry god carried out in an effort to get compliance from the survivors. For my part, I do NOT believe such notions. The GOD that I understand a little about does not DO this to anyone. These events are NOT judgments against anyone. They are natural events that have taken place on this earth for millions of years; long before humans made their appearance here. Just look at the sedimentary strata standing on edge in the Rocky Mountains or the cataclysm that killed off the dinosaurs. At the end of the Mesozoic period it is estimated that a meteorite several kilometres in diameter hit the earth and produced what is now called the "K. T. Extinction." Tidal waves and dust that blocked the sun and cooled the earth brought death on every side. This earth, as are all of us, is in transition all the time. God does not stand still, and life moves on in an endless cycle. This is the process by which God does that which God does.

However, in our blindness and fear based thinking, we still look for reasons and in our guilt we create theological explanations that imply that we could have changed these effects had we been more "righteous."

We still carry this thinking forward in our theology to some degree. Only by blood can this angry god be appeased. "He" demands the sacrifice of someone or some thing to assuage his anger. Remember the virgin and the volcano? Failing this he may go into another tantrum. I would call this idea an accusation that God acts on displaced anger: not a good thing according to modern psychiatry. I have heard ministers proclaim that "it is a fearful thing to fall into the hands of an angry God." This of course is a play on the words found in Hebrews in 10:31 in the King James bible which says living rather than angry. This appeals to those who think that people can be scared into good living. It also assumes that the one doing the scaring knows for sure what good living is.

However if God IS, then we are always in Gods hand. It is only the "anthropomorphic god" that we need fear.

The anthropomorphic god is the god of our creation. That is we invented it out of our imagination. I believe that every person walks in their own way and after the image of their own god. This god was created in their imagination. This god like the Hebrew god was "local. 2 "He" had a throne and servants, just like the kings of their day. Mark Twain remarked that "in the beginning , God created man in His own image and man has been returning the compliment ever since." What a sad but true commentary. It is no marvel to me that many clear thinking people of good conscience just say "there is no God" or opt out of formal religion. They choose to mind their own business leaving all this behind. The reality is that there is no god like the one that was presented to them. What I suspect is that they are really saying "the man made god that we are told about is nothing to worship, revere or love." While I do believe in God I certainly do not believe in such a superstitious and tribal notion as being scared into heaven, or being favoured by The Divine. Nor do I believe in the "man made god" so many seem to worship.

I could say "GOD IS" and leave it at that. However I think that I can say more than this. I have certain beliefs about God, however limited these may be, I still find them essential to my philosophy of life.

God is omnipotent, 3 omniscient 4 and omnipresent. 5 Omnipotent means all powerful. However God has delegated some power to us and therefore has placed a small limit on "ITs'" own power. To change that would mean that God was not stable, too much like us to be God. However, God reserves the right to evaluate and judge in the end. Thus my freedom is curbed and

8

limited to a specified place and time.

Omniscient means all knowing and omnipresent means all present or present everywhere. So much for the "Omnis".

These are generally accepted facts about God. However, in spite of these ideas people like to define that which they talk and think about. Defining a thing sets limits on what it is or can be. Describing God as above means that "IT" cannot be defined in a way that limits. For example, certain aspects of a tree make it clear that it is not a truck. Yet God, as "Omi" is IN both the truck and the tree. Therefore any attempt to define God must be VERY open as "all in all" for example. The Bhagavad-Gita attempts to define God in an open way. "I am the father, mother, maintainer, and grandfather of all this universe. I am what is known, I am purity, and I am the syllable om. I am the Rg. Sama and Yajur (Vedas). I am the goal, the upholder, the master, the witness, the home, the shelter and the most dear friend. I am the creation and the annihilation the basis of everything, the resting place and the eternal seed." 6

However so much of our theology conflicts with these ideas. For example we offer "prayers" that are more dictates than requests. Many of our hymns are the same. A line from one will suffice. It goes "on thy people pour thy power." 7

We say that God is IN all and then invite "HIM" (and some get really upset when they were told that God may not be male) to be present in our worship services.

The problem with trying to define God is that the infinite is not definable. If it were definable it would not be infinite. By claiming that God is male we eliminate the female. I know of no other option then, but to refer to God as "IT" no matter how remote and impersonal this may seem. Another option might be to call God "creator," or "The Divine" and these terms are also used herein.

We say that God is love and then some cheer the drowning of Pharaohs' army in the Red Sea or the destruction of Sodom. We also say that this loving God abandoned and separated Itself from humanity because of disobedience.8 Most parents are better than that. We say that God is "omnipresent" and then teach that Satan is an enemy to God. If God is indeed omnipresent then He (IT) must be present in Satan too: if Satan really does exist. Such a God is "non-local."

One definition that might partially set forth God, is to say that "God is Life." This however is only one aspect of God. This same God does not believe in the death penalty for murder if we believe the Genesis story. Why did God not kill Cain? 9 Yet our theology says that we will be killed by "him" if

10

we do not hide under the blood of the one designated to die in our place or on whom God has vented "ITs" displaced anger..

We say that God is good and then we talk about the "evil that is in the world." A world in which God is "in all and through all and above all." 10 The concept of God "in all" is, of course in conflict with what I call "separation theology." In my view God is not separate. However, in our unawareness we feel separate. Rather, it is our sense of separation, our lack of perception that generated this theory and supports it now. Being unaware of God in our lives does not make God separate. However separation theology allows us to put the blame for our sense of separation on God for expelling us from Eden. Evil is defined as that which separates us from God. Surely separation theology does this.

Must we not then define evil as "that which offends or appears to threaten our conventionally acceptable ideas or routine rather than as an entity in its' own right?" Perhaps evil is that which is different from my sense of good. As in "I don't think fires should burn people," yet fire is not a thinking phenomena as far as I know. Fire just burns whatever fuel it comes across and the heat from the fire burns whatever is close enough to be seared by it. Does this make fire evil?

11

The fact is that with the invention of Satan human kind found a scapegoat upon whom they could blame their foolish choices and angry outbursts. Actions for which they are responsible but for which they would not like to <u>accept</u> responsibility. (A scapegoat is an invention of ancient peoples who sent a goat out to die and symbolically they placed their sins on it before it was released.)<u>11</u>

Blame is one of the follies of modern humanity. The reality is that there is usually enough blame to go around to all. However fixing blame does not solve any problem.

All that blame accomplishes is to allow the blamer to feel innocent. Of course this is only a false innocence. Only by correcting the cause can the problem be solved.

I see the need to believe in an organizer and Maker. A Power that oversees all things.

I see this "maker" as God. My understanding of God is such that I do not see "IT" being concerned about what name IT should be called by. One source suggests "I AM He WHO IS." <u>12</u> Or God is "THAT WHICH CAUSES TO BE." One translation simply says I Am "The LIVING GOD" <u>13</u> Might not this be the best name, if you must have a name. Also this creator or source is NOT dependant on any of us. We are the dependant ones. If I, or we fail to supply the creator with something IT will not be hurt. Only our earthly kings and rulers are in need of something from us.

God is a title. If I choose to call IT Allah or Jehovah or Yahweh or Vishnu or Lord Krsna what does it matter? Are these not all references to the "mystery" that we title God? Yet this "mystery" is accepted as source by all those who follow and use all the names I have suggested. The fact that all these groups (religions) have different theories about "The Divine" is evidence of the infinite nature and extent of the Divine reality. It is also an indication of the degree to which human thinking has overshadowed any true knowledge of God. It is not necessarily evidence of their "heathenistic superstition" as people of some faiths might like to imply.

Is it not appropriate to attempt, however feebly, to understand something about this POWER, how IT works and how we might align ourselves with IT to our benefit? This does not mean that God plays favourites. This power is like water power, it was always there but only when people learned to harness it did it benefit human kind. Like the water power it reaches out to us in any way that we allow. Water power or the rivers flushed away waste long before flush toilets. God reaches out by supplying us with food air and all the elements required for life. It is different from water power in

13

that it works to our benefit to some degree even if we remain ignorant of it. It is like waterpower in as much as it works according to law and violation of the law could result in death. Death, in this sense, is not due to sin but rather the consequence of a foolish or misguided choice. However this may be a very good definition of sin.

The idea of special-ness as in specially loved and cared about or superior does not fit for my concept of the Divine. It does not appear that it squared with Jesus' idea either as he commented that "God makes the sun to shine on the good and the evil and the rain falls on the just and the unjust."14 This of course is not the picture presented when the Hebrew tribal god is described in the Old Testament.

In fact the idea of special-ness is one of the major sources of strife and controversy in the world of today. The ancient Israelites thought that they were special, the Nazis thought that they were "superior" or special. Most religions think that they have the inside track with God. They seem to think that they are special to God. Primitive tribes still tend to believe that accidents and wild animal attacks are acts of an angry god rather than errors in their own way of doing things. This notion of special-ness blocks the vision of brotherhood that I believe God wants us to get. It also closes us

14

to ideas that do not conform with our concepts of a God who holds us as special. It is the root of religious intolerance and most wars. From the idea of special-ness also comes the reason to fear in case we are not on the inside track with God. The concept of God held by many of the Old Testament writers was of a tribal God who lived in a house or tent that they built for "him" and who did not care that the Egyptians were drowned in The Red Sea or that "one hundred and eighty five thousand of Sennacheribs' people were killed at the gates of Jerusalem.15 In fact this event proved to them that they were special. Moreover, in their thinking, God did not care for the Assyrians, so had no trouble to kill them off.

The Israelites thought that these events should make their enemies fear them because their god was so much a god of war and so they were, or liked to think they were invincible. (This in spite of their noted commandment, "thou shalt not kill." 16) When they were defeated in battle their "prophets" told them it was a judgment of God against them due to their lack of faithfulness to their God. They had guidelines for going to war in the name of their god.17 They also were colour conscious and that attitude of theirs is often used by extremists (I refuse to call them fundamentalists) to justify racism in our day.18

15

Fear is the enemy of healthy faith. It is also the enemy of love. Hate grows from a root in fear. It also grows very close to the place where love grows. I think that people are unique and all different but equally loved and important in the eyes of The Divine. In reality we can divide the world into two groups: those who love and those who fear. Unfortunately this line is not easily drawn as most of us tend to love our friends and fear our perceived enemies. Therefore we, or most of us fall into the category of those who fear. People who fear are suspicious, on guard and uneasy. If you doubt that you fall into this category, let me ask you how often do you go out and leave your house open or un-locked?

Such ideas are new to some folks but are more clearly needed now in a "global village" or a shrinking world. To think that those we describe as Third World are of less importance because they do not have military power is foolish as the U. S. found out to their dismay in Vietnam.

Lest anyone think that I am saying that "I am God" let me put your mind at rest. Years ago I stood on a cliff looking out to the North Atlantic. I was in Newfoundland and the waves roared in. They crashed on the rocks and the spray rose a hundred or more feet up to wet my face.

That spray was produced as the waves of water were forced against the rocky shore by mighty winds. I am like that spray. Let me suggest that, in this story the ocean represents an aspect of God. Each droplet of water represents one of us. Every droplet of that spray was ocean, weak and powerless on its own and surely going to return to its home in the ocean in time. Some by a circuitous route through evaporation and condensation as snow on an artic glacier where many years would pass before it could melt and return to its true home. Other droplets would strike the cliff and pour down returning to their source in minutes. (The reality is that in this illustration the whole earth and its' atmosphere are representing God. The notion of separation from God is an illusion that is not seen by God.19

God is home for all of us how ever far we roam or how ever long we are away.) Some of that water might condense as rain in Alberta and eventually flow through the great rivers of the continent before returning, perhaps to the Hudson Bay. Is not all the water in the "Seven Seas" the same water? I Am like that droplet of water, power is not my strong feature but I Am of the same stuff as God, as all things are. In this illustration we also see that, like the water we do not "pass away," we only transform or make a transition to another place or state. We are never separated from God.

I am persuaded that there is One Mind one Power and One source from which all things flow. 5 It is the Power by which I live and breathe.

I know that this source is in and through all things. Therefore "IT" is within me and I Am one with IT even in my unawareness.

It sustains and maintains my life from day to day even in my ignorance.

I now claim this truth as the truth of my being. I open my mind to receive it now. As I learn to tune in to this power my awareness increases and my life is enriched.

I allow this as my truth with all the implications that it carries.

I rejoice in it and accept it and let it be so for me now.   And So It Is.

1. New American Bible St Joseph Medium size edition 1968-70 Genesis chapter one P. 4a.
2. Exodus 25: 8 & 17-22 New Century Youth bible 1991 by Word Publishers.
3. Genesis 17:1.
4. Daniel 2:20-22.
5. Ephesians 4:5-6.
6. Bhagavad-Gita As It Is chapter 9:16-19 Translated by A. C. Bhaktivedanta
        The Bhaktivedanta Book Trust Abridged Edition.

7. God of Grace and God Of Glory Harry Emerson Fosdick 1878-1969
8. Genesis 3:16-24. New Century Bible.
9. Genesis 4:8-15.
10. Ephesians 4:5-6
11. Leviticus 16:7-10 New Century bible.
12. Ungers' Bible Dictionary 1961 Moody Press
13. Exodus 3:14 Holy Bible translated from the Aramic by George Lamsa
14. Matthew 5:43-47.
15. Isaiah 37:36-37.
16. Exodus 20:13 King James Bible.
17. Deuteronomy 20: chapter.
18. Genesis 9:20-27.
19. Psalms 139:1-12

Two: The Triune GOD

It is to be noted that some folks go for numerology and think three is a complete number. Thus God, as complete must be triune.

One of the major differences that separates Islam from "Christianity" is the concept of "trinity." This, Islam sees as "three gods" while they affirm that there is only ONE whom they call Allah. Remember that Islam comes from the same root as Judaism as does Christianity. Is it possible that both could be right? The great advance that Israel and Judaism get credited with was the concept of ONE GOD. 1 This was probably first taught in Egypt by the Pharaoh Akhnaton and Moses likely learned this from the Egyptians, even if Israel got the credit in the Western World.2

However allowing God to be God, may it not be possible that God can accept various forms or titles? Would this not be more likely as different people with different ideas and words tried to describe their experience with The Divine. Might these forms or titles include "Father, Son and Holy Spirit? Remember the Blind men who went to see the elephant.3

Christians speak of "God the Father, God the Son and God the Holy Ghost or Holy Spirit." I would like to offer a different sequence. How about God The Father or Thinker, the Mover, God the Holy

Spirit (Mother) or FORMLESS from which all form is created and God the Son or the form created from the formless by the power of the fathers' thought ?" This would square with Pauls' thinking. 4 Perhaps these are only aspects of the same Divine Being. God is One but with more than one aspect. Just as people look different in profile than from the front or behind. If I returned to the ocean illustration I find that it also has three faces. These are water vapour, liquid water and ice. In addition to this; would not such a nebulous entity need to adopt some form that was at least partly understandable, to the very limited capacities of human kind, if it wished to communicate to humans?

The beauty of this idea is in its' simplicity.

Jesus commented that "God is spirit--" 5 However I think that spirit is a nebulous word.. That is it has a variety of meanings. For some it is the inner voice that warns and prompts 6 (The Holy Spirit) for others it is the attitude or mind set that can move a second rate sports team to play beyond its true capability and beat more highly rated competitors. While both of these ideas refer to a formless thing, I am not talking of the Holy Spirit as the voice of God in this context. I would refer to that inner urging as the voice of God or the THOUGHT of God. For my purpose here the

Spirit is the formless from which all form is made. God; by thinking forms into the formless, creates form. Thus God is "in and through and around all things." Further than that God is LIFE or awareness and so IS in all things. However the infinite God is not limited to life. It is only one aspect of the Deity. Life however is one easy way for us to see God in each other and in daily life.

In the Genesis creation myth, (remember that a myth, in this sense is not a fairy tale but a work of fiction designed to reveal a deep and mysterious truth) we are told that there was no form, I am not talking of the Holy Spirit as the voice of God in this context. I would refer to that inner urging as the voice of God or the THOUGHT of God. For my purpose here the Spirit is the formless . 7 From this formless stuff God brought forth:

1. Light,

2.Solid material (Earth)

3. From the solid material was brought forth ALL THINGS.

("The Creator made (was) one. This one became two. The two produced three and from these three all human kind descended.") 8 Based on inscriptions found in ancient sites.

This same myth, the Geneses story, tells us that we are in the form and likeness of God, the root of the anthropomorphic god idea, no doubt. However if

22

we accept the story as myth rather than take it literally, it reveals a great deal. Firstly, God sees in the dark and decides (thinks) about what "IT" would desire to have. So THOUGHT is the first step in creation.(God would be too wise to speak before "IT" thought, would IT not?) This makes thought "The Father." We often say "thought is father to the deed."

Is "spirit" not considered formless and also alive? So from the "Formless" or Spirit, some would call it "the field of infinite possibilities," God created Form.

Form then, is the "Son" of Thought and Spirit. I know that this is a radical departure from conventional thinking. Yet conventional thinking has only produced war, hatred, fear and claims of "special-ness" in our world to date. We must note here that we have not said that the formless is inert or that the form is inert. It seems to me that life and intelligence are inherent in all three. Conventional thinking allows us to "rape our earth" (our home and our little space ship) with the idea that we are superior or special and therefore have a right to what we can take. (This thinking also denies any life or sensitivity to the earth.) However the earth is not inert but alive. We rape her at the expense of future generations. Consider this thought, "we do not inherit our world from

23

our ancestors but rather we borrow it from our children." Might our children be left with nothing but a deficit? Also, if God is in all things IT must also be in the earth. In which case the earth is alive. Like any living thing, when diseased it must shake off the disease or perish. Do you think that we might be a disease plaguing the earth?

The "Divine Trinity" as listed above makes it easy to understand how God can be in all things. It also shows us how we are children of God. It shows us our freedom. God has set the system up in such a way that at some time all parts will be recycled so nothing is ever lost. Further than that, it tells us that God is IN us. The idea of separation found in the Genesis myth does not square with the infinite God. The infinite is without bounds. Therefore It MUST be in all things. (In this case God is in you too. Our problem is our unawareness.)

What a brilliant system. Only a supremely intelligent being could have figured it out. That being is GOD.

This is the reason that I refer to God as "IT " God is not male or female. Rather God is "ALL IN ALL." However you must remember that any truth can be conveyed only in terms that the hearer of that truth can comprehend. One can not do algebra before understanding simple arithmetic. This because the principles and language of arithmetic are fundamental to algebra. Ancient peoples had no language for describing God in any way except power and what active power is more expressive than Father or King? Space travel atoms and electricity were all unheard of. People who thought the earth was flat could be quite satisfied with a tribal or local God. The idea that the earth was much smaller than the sun and spun on its' axis was ridiculous to them. Thus the God of the O. T. was described in terms that contributed something to those people. We are being careless if we think they had the whole picture. In the twenty first century this Old Testament understanding is inadequate.

We are not yet aware enough to create from the formless. We are "secondary" creators. We create new forms from already existing form. Trees are formed by God but we reform the trees into lumber and the lumber into buildings and furniture. We reform iron ore into steel and so on. We also tend to think that wood and steel are both solid. Yet our physicists tell us that far from being solid both wood and steel are composed of sub-atomic particles that spin and dance in orderly fashion and that there is far more space than solid in any so called "solid."

Taking it a step further, some of our leading physicists have remarked that the universe is more like a great thought than a great machine.

Quantum mechanics is a theory based on the idea that elementary particles have both wave and particle types of behaviour. Are not waves approaching formless? The reality is that these particles can act as either wave or particle. Certain waves as x-rays for example are not blocked by all solids. Certain particles have been shown to go through two slits at the same time. 9 A trick one might expect from a wave but not from a particle. If waves can turn into particles then such waves can be re-formed into matter or matter into waves. We may be reaching very close to the point where we can understand HOW God does what "IT" does Only by thinking outside the box can we ever hope to understand The Divine. When we limit our thinking to beginnings and endings and the limits of matter as most of us understand it we have fenced ourselves in. God does not fit inside any fence or any definition that places limits on "IT." The only word that works for me is INFINITE and that implies "No Limit." No limit also implies no beginning and no end or endless.

It seems to me that Thought is capable of infinite variation. Certainly formless is infinite and form can take an infinite number of shapes.

It is clear that we live in a mysterious universe. Some of this mystery is imposed on us by our own limiting ideas. Because some sage from the past did not teach such things does not mean they are not so. Were not the teachings of those sages watered down as they passed through the hands of the so called experts? Most great teaching is.

One of the things we place great value on is our traditions. Perhaps in their place traditions are of value. However when they begin to limit us in our thinking, imagination or possible practices, tradition becomes a strait jacket. Not that any imaginable idea should be practiced but could it not be examined? At least one philosopher and thinker has said that "God is more complicated than we can think." 10 What could limit our thinking besides our tradition? Science Fiction has been based on thinking outside the box. The wildest of imaginations have been given play here. Yet how often have these stories been somewhat paralleled by subsequent events? Jules Verne's' Nautilus as described in his novel "Twenty Thousand Leagues Under The Sea" became a reality with the modern submarine for one example.

New inventions often come from young persons who as yet do not know what they "can't do." People who think outside the box are often dismissed as dreamers. Sometimes they are hailed as geniuses after they die when their dreams are more valued.

This Divine Trinity of thought, formless and form seem to me to encompass all things. Might this shed some light on the processes by which God does that which God does.

Humankind of course is not a primary creator. We are secondary creators. That is we take matter that is already formed and re-form it. Thus our creative process differs from that of God. God creates form from the formless and the form becomes son. Do we not, at times, describe certain buildings or certain theories as "the child or brain child" of so and so, their designer? The sequence is thought applied to the formless equals form. We create new form from already existing form so our process is thought, re-form and new form.

I know that things come in threes as in Spirit, Mind and Body or water ice and steam.

I know that this is a shadow of the Divine Trinity.

I know that I Am a secondary creator and that as I move further into awareness I will be more in tune with the Divine. I Am one with IT now even in my unawareness!

My life is expanded accordingly and I open myself to deeper and greater understandings.

I seek to co-operate with the Divinely guided evolutionary process.

28

My life is enriched, my horizon widens and I Am
blessed as I walk into the light.
This is the truth of my being, And so it is.

1. Deuteronomy 6:4
2. See Akanaton of Egypt on internet article by Kate
Strange "The Heretic and His City."
3. See Appendix # 1.
4. Ephesians 4:5-6 & Acts 17:24-28.
5. John 4:24.
6. 1 Kings 19:12-13
7. Genesis 1:2
8. James Churchward in "The Children of Mu. P.38 Paper
Back Library 1965.
9. The Elegant universe P. 31-33 and 102-103 by Brian
Greene, Vantage Books
10. Deepack Chopra

Three: Freedom

Freedom of choice is the birthright of all human beings. Not only that but it is a REQUIREMENT of life. We are forced to choose many times a day. Most of these choices are relatively unimportant. Some are turning points in the life of the choice maker.

Human kind like to think that they are free. However we are free only within certain limits. Even God is not totally free. God cannot make a square circle or a round triangle. By definition a circle is round and a triangle has three sides. Human kind is limited by at least these same limitations. In addition we are not as yet able to control life, although we seem quite able to determine the time of physical death for many forms of life.

One of the big difficulties we have is with our belief systems. <u>One of the major blocks to changing beliefs is holding opinions as "knowledge" without examining the facts.</u> It seems to me that most world religions do this very thing. A few examples include the Jews looking back to Moses as the final authority. Islam looks back to Mohamed, Christians to Jesus, some of the "Eastern Religions" look back to the writings of Arjuna as delivered to him by "Lord Sri Krsna," the name here used for God. In always looking back for final answers to life issues are we not "walking backwards into the future?" Not only that but while human nature still needs healing, the physical circumstances of life today bear no resemblance to the circumstances of life for Moses or even of Jesus. While Moses may have had the clearest revelation of God in O. T. times and Jesus the most accurate in N. T. times we know more of the LEGEND of Jesus than of the real man. We also know more about disease, sexual deviation and the world in which we live than did folks of those days. As long as we insist on our exclusive religions, which look back and are thus trapped in superstition and fear, our world will not heal. Why look backward?

I have never seen a football player or a hockey player who deliberately runs or skates backward against the opposing defence. He may get turned around in the rough and tumble of the play but he always faces the opposition when he starts out. Perhaps some of our religious leaders could take a lesson. However we are free to continue as we are if we so choose. That is our God given right. We can choose it even if it does not work. Human kind is, after all, perhaps the most stubborn of all creatures.

The reality is that we are bound by tradition and

31

the attitude that "we have never done it this new way before." Speaking only of "Christian" thought processes as I understand them; if Jesus was the last word on God then my assumption that God is infinite goes down the drain. However Jesus did say that he had more things to say that they (we) were not ready for yet (now). 1 He promised his "friends" a "guide" for their path. Too often we substitute the wisdom of our own education and our smarts for the :guide" offered by Jesus. Are we ready for that guide today?

Surely an infinite God does not ever run out of words, ideas or creative endeavours. If IT did would IT not cease to be infinite? If we are progressing, and we are in some ways, do we not need some updating from time to time? We are good at updating where technology is concerned yet we often refuse to update our belief systems. We update when we start to learn about computers. The assumption, in religious circles, seems to be that we have a final and complete system given long ago. To make any change would be a disservice to God. The consequence is that many thinking people write off the whole idea of God as superstition as already pointed out.

We create our own future by the choices that we make daily. Some people are so stuck on the idea of freedom that they actually imprison themselves in their version of freedom. By determining to live by their own rules they become slaves to those rules. They refuse to conform because it might limit their freedom. At times this refusal to conform blocks their own growth. Have many folks not imprisoned themselves in old ideas, ideas that are no longer valid? To be truly free I must always be able to choose a course of action based on its merits now. And this whether it requires me to agree (conform) to your idea or my old idea or to choose a different path. Some times conformity may be wise. Abiding by the laws that protect us all, as in driving on the right in North America is an example. However we would drive on the left to pass a parked vehicle or a slow moving vehicle if the left was clear. We are flexible about this rule. So we assume the chains that bind and limit us by our predisposition to "know" without proper examination. Tradition, habit and precedent are three of these chains.

Note that the Jew, Viktor Frankel comments that he had more freedom in the concentration camp than did the Nazi guards that ran the place 2 Why? Because even with the privations and indignities that he suffered including the starvation he was free to think while they did what they were told. They were not allowed, or chose not to think for themselves, so they thoughtlessly obeyed.

Is it not interesting that Jesus remarked that "the condemnation was that light had come into the world and men loved (preferred) darkness?" 3 Might it be that part of that love of darkness was the freedom from new ideas? Might new ideas upset the status quo? Do we not generate theories that seem to explain our lives and then take comfort in them? Do we not then proclaim that these theories throw light (understanding) on our situation? I think we do and we compound the situation by getting stuck in these partial truths.

Light comes in many forms some of which are not visible to the naked eyes. Light is a form of radiation and in radiation we have infra red rays, gamma rays, radio waves etc. all of which are light but not visible to the naked eye. However I doubt that this kind of light was in Jesus mind when he made that remark. I think he was referring to information. I think that people were, in effect saying to him, "do not confuse me (us) with facts, my (our) minds are made up." However even light as we see light with our naked eyes does some very peculiar things. Light is said to travel at a speed of 186,000 miles per second. According to this theory if I were traveling at 100,000 miles per second and you shone a light from behind me it would pass me at only 86,000 miles per second. (I have no idea how these experiments were done but such an experimen was performed). To the surprise of the experimenter the light was measured at a speed of 186,000 miles per second as it passed or in other words it passed him as if he were standing still. Perhaps light is more Divine than we think. It has been said that light acts more like thought than like a thing.

In view of the fact that so much "light" is around us and yet unseen why do we choose to deny the possibility that other, as yet un-detected things also surround us? Visible light is a very small sliver of the radiation spectrum. This includes Electric waves, Radio waves, Infra-red waves, Visible light, Ultra-violet waves, X-rays, Gamma rays and secondary Cosmic waves.

Sound is another element that exists beyond our ability to hear. Sound waves that vibrate above or below the frequency of our hearing range are non-existent to us yet we know they do exist. Dogs hear a wider range of frequency than do humans.

If God is free and human kind is even a faint model of the original then we must be free. Only in freedom can we learn to fly. The down side of this freedom is that in learning to fly, (what ever flying means to you), we must also be free to crash. It is often our fear of crashing that blocks our progress. This is the one big drawback to freedom; we have to accept responsibility for our choices and our actions. Too many of us would rather blame than accept responsibility. We seem to miss the point that freedom and responsibility are locked together and are inseparable. How would Robert Fulton have ever built a steamship or Alexander Graham bell the telephone if they had listened to those who "knew" that such things were impossible? They had to be free to fail. And fail they did, many times. When Thomas Edison was told by his assistant that "we can't make a light bulb, it cant be done," after about a thousand failures, Edison replied "It can be done but now we know another way that won't work."

War is one of the arguments put up by the non-believers. If God was love "He" IT would not allow war. (Do we not have a clear directive against war among the Ten Commandments?) However where is your freedom or mine if we are not allowed to war if we so choose? More than this, we often hear people say "He/She MADE me do--" Where is your freedom if I, or someone else can MAKE you do anything? The fact is that you CHOOSE. I may be able to make it very easy for you to choose a certain line of action. (Remember in the movie The God Father, he made an offer that could not be refused His theory was do as I say or die.) When this offer was made to Jesus he chose to die. Jesus in fact refused the "offer that could not be refused." I may even be able to make it almost impossible to choose differently.

However there are always alternatives and you or I give away our power when we allow another to MAKE us do--. Martin Luther King. Mahatma Gandhi and numberless nameless soldiers, heroes; have refused the offer that could not be refused. God does not deprive us of our freedom in this way. When I say "you MADE me--" I am laying blame. Laying blame is a psychological ploy to allow me to feel blameless. The trouble is that this ploy is a lie. If I drink myself to death it was my hands and my fingers that held the glass. If I shoot someone it was my hands that held the gun. I am ultimately responsible for all my choices as an adult. I may be pre-programmed to an extent as a child by my upbringing and my family values. As an adult it is my duty to examine this pre-programming and choose that part which fits for me. Failure to do so does not relieve me of the accountability for my actions. It is part of the price of being an adult and being free. Some of the ideas that my Father had are not acceptable in the twenty first century. In just the same way some of my ideas will not be acceptable in the twenty second century. They may be too advanced for now and too limited then; or some may be just plain foolish. Is the principle of freedom and responsibility not advocated by those who argue that God had to do something to "save" human kind from the mess they were in? Was this mess not the result of God giving them freedom? We even hold this principle in law. If you dig a pit and do not adequately fence and guard it you will be held responsible for the injury to anyone who falls into it. Our theological leaders have spent a lot of time making God responsible. They have even gone to the trouble of inventing a scapegoat. They say that Jesus is the scapegoat and Gods' anger was directed to him rather than to those who deserved it but "claim the name of Jesus." This thinking is based on the idea that God is angry and that only blood can turn away that anger. It is even argued that this is a sample of Gods' justice. Frankly I see no justice in punishing one person for the crimes of another. It also implies that some elements of life do disappear into nothingness thus denying the principle that every act has an effect and that we must "reap what we sow."4

It also implies that God can misdirect "ITs" anger and take it out on an innocent: an action not accepted as proper among reasonable folks.

The thing is that God was smarter than that. It made all things cycle so nothing is ever lost. If Jesus showed us anything it was that physical eath is not the end of all things for humankind.

Death is only a transition to a different level of awareness. Jesus came back to report; and prove the truth of this statement.

I doubt that God decided that Jesus must come and die. Sinful, headstrong and envious or fearful people made this decision. God allowed them the freedom to do away with the radical. But the All Wise God always has a plan "B" and more if needed. Now God could use Jesus not only to show the light, but also through his death, to demonstrate that life IS eternal. One of Gods' skills is turning stumbling blocks into stepping stones. However we must be willing to use them as stepping stones or we will still see them as stumbling blocks.

With our limited vision we tend to think that this life is all there is. Therefore we cling to it grimly and see death as a terrible enemy. This fear is one of the great chains that rob us of freedom. Jesus resurrection could have freed us from this fear. It does if we choose to allow ourselves to believe the story.

People of faith from almost all religions are taught that death is only for the body. However with our limited vision most people pay more lip service that solid action to the concept of life beyond the grave. The reality is that death is a transition and not THEE end.

Consider the life cycle of the dragonfly. It starts out as an egg, hatches (makes a transition) into a little worm or nymph that lives in the water. At the right time this nymph will swim to the surface and go through another transition. (At this point the nymph is dead to the nymphs that remain in the muck down below.) When the transition is complete it will be a dragon fly. This adult dragonfly cannot return to satisfy any possible curiosity among the remaining nymphs. It is no longer equipped to swim or draw oxygen from water. How could the dragonfly explain air and sunlight to the nymphs (worms) in the muck at the bottom of the pond? It now lives in a totally different world, a world that is beyond the experience of the former creature that is was. Is not our life, like that of the dragon fly, an event that carries on after our transition?

Of course all these statements are faith based, as we do not see what lies beyond the door of our own transition. The dragonfly may or may not be a parallel to our own case. We can only speculate or not as we choose. Basically any position that we take is a faith statement. However we do have the evidence from physics and observation that nothing is destroyed, only changed in form. It Seems to me that it is a longer reach to make the faith statement that there is nothing beyond the grave than it is to say there is existence beyond.

Remember the dragon fly, so much different from the nymph but still alive and well.

I think the adage "as below so above" has merit in this case. However above may imply a geographic location and that is not required for the principle to be true. Above could be interpreted as on a higher level of awareness.

Awareness comes at several levels. The lump of granite does not seem to have awareness at all. However the atoms that spin and dance within the granite are aware of each other.

This is how they keep the rock in its same form. Plants seem to be more aware. They can turn toward the light. In the animal kingdom we can see the awareness of the coyote as he hunts and the awareness of the rabbit as he flees from the hunter. We like to think that humans are the only animal that can reason logically. My personal opinion is that those who think like that have no experience with horses, dogs etc. Yet humans seem more advanced in the art of abstract thinking. Some would say that we are "aware of our awareness." We could say that what we have outlined here is a rising scale of awareness. Humans being at the top. The next question is how much higher can the scale go? Perhaps there is no top limit.   If God is unlimited maybe this ladder has no top limit. This would certainly leave room for more advances and more progress at the human level.

I see that I Am free in the freedom that is Gods' gift to me. I Am free to be selective in my thoughts, discriminating in my tastes and deliberate in my actions. I know that I am responsible for my choices, how I deal with my anger and for my results.

I Am one with God. There is no line where I stop and God starts as IT is IN all.

I move forward in this awareness. My horizons expand and great things for my good occur in my life and experience. I am filled with joy.

My life is enriched and my understanding grows in amazing ways I give thanks and allow it to be so now for me. And So It Is.

1. John16:7-12 The Holy Spirit promised in John 14:15-17.
2. Viktor Frankel "Mans Search For Meaning"
3. John 3:17-19.
4. Galatians 6:7.

Four: Evolution

Evolution is seen by those who argue against it, as a theory that rules God out. I think that evolution is the process by which God does that which God does. For example, the Model T Ford is a long way short of the modern computer timed Ford of the twenty first century. Has the Ford not evolved? Would it have evolved naturally if Ford (human) intelligence had not been applied to the process? Some will argue that it is still an automobile but I say "that the automobile has now many relatives including trucks, tractors and even aero planes and perhaps even rocket ships that spring from the same root as the model T." May the model "T" not itself have evolved from the horse drawn buggies of an earlier era: or perhaps even from the invention of the wheel? May it not also have already evolved into support for the evolutionary process to bring about good things? (Like safer and more reliable transportation.) Perhaps even in spite of evolution being seen as a bad word in many religious circles we have been blessed by it.

The technology and metallurgy that enable the modern car also enable the other advances in modern engineering.

In this context some would argue that God does not exist. They would say that the idea of God is only for the weak who cannot face the reality of immanent oblivion in death. Yet I see the so called "Godless scientists" identifying "LAWS" which they describe as firm e. g. the "law of gravity." The fact is that all our so called progress in physical terms of engineering etc. are based on the truth and reliability of these laws.

I made my living for years as a shift supervisor in a high pressure steam plant. Here we dealt with power, pressure and electricity that was far more powerful than any man or set of men. The only reason that we could control these massive forces was that they obeyed certain laws. All we had to do was know the laws that governed electricity, steam, combustion and steel and we could control the plant. The laws were learned over many years and at the cost of many lives. When anyone broke any one of these laws they were in grave danger of paying with their health or their life. We burned billions of cubic feet of natural gas every year without harm to any of the crew because the fire obeyed the law. My BIG question is WHO MADE THE LAW? Our processes were repeatable because the law required it of the physical elements. To me the existence of these laws requires that there be a "LAW GIVER."

Is all this not driven by intelligence? Are we as people not using the same process as does God? If the Ford cannot progress without guidance why do

44

some insist that the universe can progress without guidance? I for one say that it can not. By the way, does the Ford not also obey these same laws?

If we look again at the Genesis myth we will find that it shows a progression from light to human life. The first chapter of Genesis is clear on this point. The story gets clouded later on.

It is not clear how much freedom of choice is implanted into the beasts of the field and fowls of the air. However the Creation Myth does clearly state that humans have choice. Might this change our understanding of the way evolution works? If we do in fact have choice then must we not co-operate if further progress is to be made? Some folks even think that we are co-creators with God. How can we co-create if we do not co-operate? Is it not evident that we have a responsibility to "Mother Earth?"

May it be that the human race has progressed to the point where "Love Or Perish" as Dr. Smiley Blanton suggests in his book of the same name, 1 is a definite reality? Our freedom may allow us to go as far as destroying our "civilization." May it be that we can also use our intelligence to solve our issues and thus make a break through to the dreamed of Utopia? Is it possible that we can join together to create peace, health and true freedom for all folk? If we go back to the evolution of the automobile we can see that as learning increased (usually from previous mistakes) new and better models evolved. Is it not possible that human kind could learn from past events (history) and so make wiser and more "life supporting: decisions in future times. Remember that the future is as close as the next second of time and the choices that support the future are made in the NOW. History need not repeat if we are willing to change our choices. Different choices will produce different results.

Even in our personal life our growth follows an evolutionary path. There are four stages and possibly more to come. (a) These are the absolute wonder and faith of a little child.

Everything is new and there is wonderment and awe in every experience. Some folks never get past this stage. (b) The next stage is the "knowing stage." When people act and seem to think they know it all. It requires some learning. It is often seen in teens and early stages of adulthood. Some folks that get past the first stage get stuck in this one. They seem to take the position that "I know, my mind is made up so do not confuse me with alternative ideas." In some cases it is opinion with out study or thought, as in "the bible says and that is it for me." (c) The third stage is disillusionment and cynicism. When the perceived answers of stage two do not provide the satisfaction required to deal with severe life trauma or disasters. Many folks who have survived war and natural disasters get to this stage and get stuck. (d) The fourth stage, for those who reach it, is somewhat similar to stage one. There is amazement and wonder mixed with awe. However there is a maturity that marks a distinct difference from stage one. The folks in stage four can say "even if we do not understand, yet we have faith and believe that our wonderful universe is no accident. A Power greater than ours is at work and we believe there is a purpose."

These stage four folks can usually give a thoughtful reason for their faith and hope. There may be a fifth stage beyond these but only a very few have ever reached it: Jesus and a few only.

Up to now our physical evolutionary progress has been in things. The worlds of chemistry engineering and physics are examples. Some progress has been made in interpersonal relations as we have moved from singleness to family, tribe and nation. It seems to me that these steps were taken in a rather conscious manner. We have also moved in an attempt to provide through law, security against those among us who refuse to co-operate in securing the general welfare of society. Surely these steps have been halting and many efforts have led to dead ends yet our intelligence has been applied and progress has been made. Can we continue to move forward into environmental, international and perhaps even extra-terrestrial relationships?

It seems to me that we have two alternatives before us. Either we can learn to love and get along or we can bring about our own destruction. Is fear not at the root of the risk of destruction? I am told that "perfect love casts out fear." 2 Our choice then is love or fear. In this context love means RESPECT. It also means caring for and being aware of the needs of others but primarily all this grows out of respect. It means respecting other peoples ideas and their opinions and treating them as equals. (Just because someone has gone to university for a number of years does not negate the life experience of another whose training ground was life itself. For example, few of us could survive for long in the Amazon Jungle if we did not learn from the folks who live there full time.) Respect for the ideas, feelings and faith of others is our only hope. Much as we may wish to deny it, not one of us has a corner on the "truth market." There is some truth in all our ideas and some error too. God is still beyond all of us and only God has THEE truth.

The question becomes, are we wise enough and alert enough as a people to solve our issues in peaceable ways or will we use our death dealing capability to destroy all? We make progress in dealing with disease but not with hunger. Hunger does not bother the rich nations: and certainly not many of the rich people to any extent, but distributing the food might cost money. Our governments, in a misguided effort to insure safety make loans to poor nations. What do they ask in return?

That the beneficiaries of this largess are required to spend at least part of the money on arms made in the country that gave the loan. Is our "charity" not based on fear, greed and the desire for power? We of the rich nations then point to our acts of charity as proof that God loves us. In this way many mainly poor peoples are armed angry and HUNGRY all at the same time. Their anger arises from fear. Is this not a recipe for disaster? Can you blame parents for acting to try and save their starving children? What would you do if your child were, not hungry, but starving?

Are not parents the same all over the world? What do they want for their children? Something better than they had, peace and safety with good health. Are these not universal wants; nay, needs of humanity? Guns, dictatorial governments and despotic rulers kept in power in third world nations by the rich nations for political or economic advantage are not what people need. Is it any wonder that activists in those backward countries come to think that the only way to free themselves from this trap is by military force? Is military force not a very short sighted and in the long run a counterproductive process? Does it not promise a "quick fix" and is that promise not a lie? And what lies at the heart of the power struggle if not fear? What stops us from seeing the futility of armed power? What stops us from seeing past the religious differences to the common human needs of all people? Probably distrust: and does distrust not also spring from fear?

Some will ask "why does God not do something to fix this? Why does "IT" not wave "Its" magic wand and solve all these problems?" To me it seems clear that God has given us freedom of choice. Then only by removing that freedom could God fix the state of affairs above mentioned. Would not the removal of freedom limit us in our personal development? Might not this limit block the possibility of our growing into appropriate "images" of God? Would we not become robots only? Would we not then be in the same state as people living under an dictatorship by an occupying army? I think that God wants more for us.

I believe that we must come to the realization of our oneness by our choice.

We are one people no matter what our skin colour or our religious or non-religious stance. I ask these questions because I am sure that if you think of the issues in this way you already know the answers. The really big question then is; when are we going to do something to change the status quo? Because "it was good enough for my father" is no justification for staying where we are now. Surely we have learned a few things over the last century.

Let us take that learning and turn it into progress for ALL humankind and not just more privilege for the few.

Is this not the message of Jesus and also the message of other great religious leaders? Even if that message is blurred and polluted by the blind thinking of lesser people this truth will shine through. We are one people, regardless of skin colour. What we do to others we do to ourselves. This is the endless cycle of life.(Is this not what Jesus meant when he said "they know not what they do?" 3) (The Jews brought about the killing of Jesus and less that 40 years later Titus destroyed Jerusalem and scattered them over a large area leaving them homeless.) The actions of the Jewish nation under their then leaders, came back on the nation in a different form. Is this not also the message of the "Golden Rule?" <u>4</u>

I am convinced that there is one mind at the centre
of all.
I believe that it is in and through all. Therefore I
am one with all things. I am one with all people
and one with the earth from which my body grows.
What I do to another I do to myself also. What I
give out is what returns to me.
I open my eyes and my understanding. I am open
to new and positive ideas. I move forward into the
light. I support the evolutionary process that opens
the way for universal brotherhood.   I refuse to fear
or to act from a fear motive. I am MIND and I
know that awareness is an act of mind and that
mind is eternal   as is spirit. Therefore I have
nothing to fear.
I rejoice in my new found freedom. I see all people
as brothers and sisters. I am one with all things. I
am of the same stuff as the stars.
I give thanks for this new understanding and I let it
be so now for me. AND SO IT IS!

1. Love or Perish Smiley Blanton M. D. Fawcet 1965
2. 1 John 4:18.
3. Luke 23:34.
4. Mat. 7: 11-12.

Five: "Sin"

Sin is a word that people do not like to hear. It arouses feelings of guilt and fear. However, sin is nothing more that that which separates us from God. Whether that separation is by design or by accident is of no consequence. If it leads us away or diverts our attention from our source and our power, it is sin. One of the damages that sin inflicts on us is the fracturing of our vision. It may be illustrated by examining a car windshield after it is hit by a stone. The wind shield is not broken but it is fractured and light is distorted so that you cannot rely on what you think you see through it. Thus with sin we have a distorted view of life and things in general. The first distortion is our sense of separation from God. If we feel separated we are separated in our minds and we will act accordingly. So some accept the fact of God being "in through and above all things" and yet think of themselves as exempt from this blanket coverage. Some are so sure they are separated from God that they see God as local and thus separate. They also disregard any argument that supports the possibility of God IN ALL. 1

When we are born into this world we find that, through our eyes, we are at the centre of our world. Which ever way we turn we find that we are central to our visible world. Our physical senses

53

and our sense of separation support this false idea. We are like the ancients who thought that the earth was the centre of the universe. And we are just as wrong. When I rely on my physical eyes I note that I am still at the centre of my world. Education will give me a broader view. However it is like climbing a pole. It gives me a broader view but I am still at the centre. My windshield is still fractured.

Human kind has made some limited progress in this matter. We have moved from ME to ME and my WIFE and on to my FAMILY and further on to my TRIBE and finally my NATION. However we certainly have rebellious elements in all of the aforementioned. Our next step forward must be to realize OUR WORLD. It is doubtful if this step can be taken while we are split and adamant on issues of God, doctrine and politics within our families, tribes and nations. It certainly cannot be attained while some elements in our world are bent on using force to have their way about religion or what ever. The physical did not show the ancients that the earth was a small dot near the periphery of the Milky Way. The physical is not always a reliable source of information. Yet many will say "if I do not see it I will not believe it." Only through the eyes of faith can I see that my world revolves around God and not me. This is to say that God calls the shots, although I would often like to do so. However I have some experience with calling the shots. When I was an infant I got instant attention when I called. If I own or manage a business I get to call some of the shots. It is easy to begin to believe that calling the shots is my right.

Apostle Paul notices this problem when he writes "I see in my body's members another law at war with the law of my mind." 2 This conflict between his wants and his knowledge, he calls sin. It identifies a split within, not only Paul but a split within all of us. This split is the burden of sin. Flowing from this is the idea that if we have a revelation; or think we have a revelation from God, we therefore know the whole mind of The Divine. This leads us to the error of thinking that our standard of values is final and our judgments upon life and morals are ultimate and final. If we do not have the revelation then we set ourselves up as the final arbiter anyway. It is said that many people believe in God and want to be involved but only in an advisory capacity.

This sin is selfish and self centred. We put ourselves in the place where God belongs. From this place we give orders; even to God. Is this not the root of our wars and fears? We each want to give the orders and in effect usurp Gods' power.

We seem to want to have the "say" and even to protect God from the error and foolish beliefs of others. As if God needs our protection. Naturally we "FEAR" God as we, unconsciously of course, have mentally unseated God. One of our great hymns is an example. "God Of Grace and God of glory--wait for it-- ON THY PEOPLE POUR THY POWER." 3 Obviously WE are acting as Gods commanders in this case.

 Or it is as if we were buttering God up to get our way. Do you not think that God has always desired to pour out "ITs'" power on anyone who qualifies? However there is a price to be paid for great power. Else this power abuses people. Are we willing and able to accept the responsibility for the exercise of Divine power? Can we administer this power with love and equality for all?

This sense of my own importance, that I am at the centre and the authority on all issues is my major sin. An example follows. I watched a little girl five years old who insisted to her mother that she "knew" even though it was apparent that she did not know. This notion that we "know" does not dissolve with years for many. We would rather be right than happy. It seems that for many of us, self worth is attached to our being right. This makes it hard to examine and re-evaluate our position. It is not deliberate. It is a natural mistake. This mistake leads me to discount God and to make my needs and wishes of paramount importance in my life. It separates me from God. In effect I am a rebel who tries to usurp Gods' place. (The bible says that whoever is a friend of the world is enemy to God.") 4 It is my basic sin. All other "sins" flow from this one and each step leads me further away from the truth; that God is the centre. Huge telescopes and careful observation have allowed learned people to see that the earth is not the centre of the universe. Careful observation and a little humility can help me to see that I am not at the centre of my world. If I were the whole thing would revolve around me. Death illness and pain would be ruled out in my world if I were at the centre. But if I were in charge how would I deal with over population? Therefore the idea that I am at the centre is false, even though my physical senses say that I am. A little intellectual effort shows the fallacy of the concept. Consider also the burdens that we place on ourselves by taking on the problems of the Universe. A friend of mine observed that it was time for her to resign as "Resident Caretaker of the Universe."

So a combination of the physical, the intellectual and faith is required to provide the best information about my world. This is a tough concept to grasp as the physical alone is still screaming that I am central. This sin is the major block to true spirituality. Most of my prayers are for my welfare. Most disregard how the benefits I ask for may impact other folks adversely. An example would be when we pray that we might overcome or convert our enemies, those of a different religion or colour. Is not this self centred notion and attitude the root of most if not all our worlds problems? It blinds us to the reality that God is IN and through ALL things and therefore is central to all. It tends to convey the notion that I or we are special. Since "WE" know they must conform to our thinking.

The fact is that God is "The Resident Caretaker of The Universe." Jesus said "my Father works-- and I work." 5 We need to relax and allow God to do "ITS" job and accept that others are not less than or more ignorant than us and therefore have fewer or even no rights. We are all equal and this is the simple lesson all must learn.

If you doubt that we want to put self in God's place and run the show just look at how we denigrate God. Some use the name in terribly disrespectful ways. Some even deny the existence of a supreme power. If, in fact such a power did not exist would this not create a "power vacuum" into which one of us might flow? This claim of the atheist, that there is no God, is the most flagrant evidence of the human desire to displace the Divine.

This concept of the centrality and non local nature of God is hinted at in the bible. We have the Psalmist saying "where ever he goes God is there." 6 We can question whether he thought that God read his mind and went there to meet him or if God was everywhere. We have Apostle Paul saying "in him we live and move and have our being." 7 Also "one God and Father of us all who is in all things through all things and above all things." 8 These ideas suggest a "NON LOCAL" entity. This non-local aspect of God is expressed in Holy Writ as is the concept of a local entity. The local is much easier to understand and again shows how we create God in our image. The local is so much easier to picture.

Beside this we have pictures of God sitting on his throne just like a human king. A concept much easier for us to grasp. It also provides a mental picture of a "LOCAL" entity. Some thing much more easily understood by humans. It is easier to grasp and much more widely held. The ancient Israelites thought of God as local. "He" sat on the mercy seat between the cherubim. 9 This however puts a limit on the Divine. It cuts "IT" down to our scale of thinking. This kind of thinking led J. B. Phillips to write a book called "Your God Is TOO

Small." 10 Might it be possible that God can assume a form at times in order to help us understand? Perhaps God is BOTH local and non-local. Might not an infinite God have that power? The god of the Old Testament is indeed too small for our modern world. "He" was a LOCAL entity. This was the concept of most of the Old Testament writers. He was conceived as taking sides in wars and showing favouritism to "special" people. This kind of thinking is at the root of most of the worlds problems to this day.   No one can be "special" in the eyes of God and we are told that God is "no respecter of persons." 11 We need some evolutionary progress in our concepts of God. All these old ideas grow out of the self centred notion that "I" or "my people" are at the centre: that we are right.. That we have a right to rape the earth and to lord it over those less powerful or less able to defend themselves for what ever reason.   It denies the concept of brotherhood and also the idea of loving ones neighbour as self.

This is the source of most of our earthly troubles. We harbour suppressed anger based on our frustration with being unable to get our way. This becomes the root of war, murder, robbery, and violence of all sorts. This false, but so clearly true to the casual observer, idea that we are, or should be, boss permeates society. We hide it so well that most do not recognize it even when it is pointed out. One of our adverse traits is the denial of that which is distasteful, to us. Thus many would deny their need for control.

When the basic premise is so far off the mark it sets up a system of error that can be called sinful. Again I say, this is not necessarily deliberate but it still leads people away from God and the truth. This then is our basic sin and the place at which basic change must occur if we are ever to SEE the "millennium," the reign of peace or the Kingdom of God. This state is the hope and the dream of human kind in all ages. Utopia, Zion, The Happy Hunting ground or what ever the dream is named in the minds of humanity. When the basic premise is wrong there is no way for the system to be successful in achieving this kingdom result..

I now realize that I am not separate in reality. This separation is only a false image that I see though my broken and shattered windshield glass. All things originate from a single source and all return to that source in an endless cycle. This source I call God and I am one with it even now.

Therefore I open myself to hear and sense the voice of God to me. I learn to see others as family. I look for the God, "LIFE," in them and see God in all. I allow people to be who they are only requiring that I be allowed the same priveledge. I examine new ideas for merit and I am patient with my self and others as we sort out differences. I learn to see God in all. I have respect for nature and for life. I make decisions that support life and freedom for all. My world view expands, my horizons recede and I move forward into the light. I am filled with hope and joy as I advance. I let it be so now and SO IT IS!

1. Acts 17:24-28.

2. Romans 7:14-24.

3. Harry Emerson Fosdick 1878-1969 "God of Grace and God of Glory"

4. James 4:4.

5. John 5:17

6. Psalm 139:7-12.

7. Acts 17:24-29.

8. Ephesians 4:5-6.

9. Isaiah 37:16. Note "the gold creatures" were the cherubim at either end of the ark of
   covenant.

10. "Your God is Too Small" J. B. Phillips Collier Books MacMillan 1961.

11. Acts 10:34. "Treats everyone the same New Century see also K. J. V.

Six: The Concept of Specialness

Specialness is a notion held by most people in some form.   The Jews used to think they were special. Most Christian denominations think that they are special.   Special as in closer to God or more loved. It tends to come out as "better than." There is even a hymn that some sing that goes something like "We belong to the Family of God." 1 The singers seem to be setting themselves apart as special. . However the family of God is much broader than any small group or sub group.   As creator of all God may be described as "Father of All." As Father of all must not the "Father" be equally concerned about all?

The fact is that we are all "unique" but none are special. We may be special to our earthly parents. Can God be partial to any one of ITs Children? We all, in the human family, have fingers. However no two fingers leave the same prints. We all have talents but no two have exactly the same mix of talents. We all have D. N. A. but not the same. We are each unique. I heard of one mother who had seven children and who remarked that she would not give ten cents for another seven like them but would not take a million dollars for any one of those she had. I suspect that she thought they were each of untold value and each unique. Was she being fair and equal in her treatment of her seven children?

I think that each one might have unique needs from time to time and need special treatment for those needs. However I saw this statement as her holding each as equal and precious.

God as "Father of All" must be equally or even more even handed must IT not? Jesus seemed to think so when He is reported to have remarked that God "makes the sun to rise on the evil and the good and the rain to fall on the righteous and the unrighteous." 2 This concept is expanded upon by James when he points out that people often make certain people special by the treatment they hand out. He says God does not do that. He calls it favouritism. He suggests that God rewards those who qualify by Gods standards. Not those who appear to men as qualified. 3

The concept of Specialness is held in some form by most if not all religious bodies. It is one of the MOST divisive concepts found in religion. It suggests that "we" have the inside track with God. Like the little girl mentioned in a previous chapter, we "know." This brings God down to our level again. If we "know" then we can argue with God and be "right."4

We have blinders on and wear them most of the time. The family of God consists of the ENTIRE creation. The beasts of the field, the plants that grow, the whole human race and even the earth on which all these grow. All this is the family of God. None of it is "special" but all of it is unique. We are not just playing with words here. Special as in favoured is a limiting and cramping concept that has no place in the mind of people who are aware. It arises from the same root as our basic sin. To think we are special requires us to put ourselves apart and above the rest. It grows in the same soil as the concept of "Right" as in "I am right." This of course makes anyone who does not agree with me "wrong" or less than. Again I have set myself up as the authority and in practical terms assumed Gods throne.

All this ignores the need for love and brotherhood. It makes for elitism and leads us to compare and pass judgments on others. The roots of war are found in this soil. The Muslim extremists are saying that they know what God wants and are going to see that God (Allah) gets what IT wants even if they have to kill the dissenters. Could not Allah do his own killing if that was what he wanted? Do not the extreme "Christians" do the same? Have they not always done the same? I guess that in the view of these extremists neither God nor Allah is capable of dealing with the rebellious. Obviously that is why they must act for their god, a poor imitation of the real GOD. Part of the enmity between Muslim and Christian stems from the Crusades. Here the "Christians" sought to force their way on the "heathens" who "desecrated the HOLY CITY." Specialness makes for privilege, favouritism and consequent hard feelings. Is not the tradition that God promised the land of Canaan to Israel the root of much strife today? Yet how could a just and fair God sacrifice one family for another? Might it not be Moses that made the promise? Might Moses have attributed this promise to God to give himself credence? This seems to be a common ploy practiced by Hitler and most priests in an effort to gain power. It is also an ego builder and a very successful effort in so many cases. The need for power stems from fear. Why was I omitted from the guest list or why was it only for the rich? Thus we have some saying "you are not good enough" and others saying "I would not company with those people anyway." Only from fear would one ask these questions. Only from fear would this matter. When one is confident in the love of God there is nothing to fear. If we think we are special we expect favours. True, in this world many do get favours due to good looks, family connection or status. Surely we can expect better than that from God.

Unless of course, we have invented God and It is no better than we are. Again it is no wonder that some thinking people dismiss the whole thing as fantasy. How could they do otherwise when God is represented in such a human way by those who claim to "know?"

Expectations set us up for fear. What if our expectations are not met? (A little self disclosure here.) I used to expect that if I belonged to the "right church" and behaved according to the teachings of said church, God would bless me. Why: because I was special. Of course this blessing was to be measured by my yardstick. A yardstick that was based on self centred thinking. (See chapter on sin.) It was a hard lesson for me to learn that such expectations were fantasy. The real world as we know it does not work that way.

Many people expect the government to make things good and perfect by law. Many people expect trouble from young men who dress and have hair dos different from the conventional. Some even expect God to make things right without their having to lift a finger to assist. They do not want to be "co-creators" with God. They want to support God but only in an advisory capacity. God should do it all seems to be their attitude. Perhaps Gods" law will prevail. However, if Gods' law does not prevail now, from what source does the law of gravity get its power? (Might Gods' law prevail but not Gods' wish?

Suppose that Gods' will is that we should have joy but when we violate the law we suffer. That is the law but not necessarily Gods desire for us.) I suspect that we will learn obedience, if need be by the things that we suffer. God might desire that we not suffer but we may not allow God a choice. If we violate the law we will pay the price.

This last is especially true for those who dream of Heaven. It seems that they expect that God will "make" people get along or perhaps "make" them conform to the expectations of the "expector" (It could not be Heaven if things were not done according to the standard of the expector, could it?) Of course this would mean that in their heaven people had no choices. Might this be how you think and imagine Heaven to be? The story is told of the traveller who arriving at "the Pearly Gates" asked for a tour. He was assigned a guide and off they went. He saw a group singing and shouting Amen in one place. Anther place he saw people prostrating themselves and praising saying "God is great." He saw some making the sign of the cross and then they came to a great wall. The traveller was shocked and asked how such a thing could be in Heaven. The guide replied " those are certain folks who think that they are the only ones here." Could Heaven really be divided and composed of such small enclaves?

This seems to me to be counter to Gods' way of doing things. If so then God would have to change. Even if God imposed peace and quiet in "Heaven" would this be different from the peace imposed by force of arms here on earth? Surely that peace is no peace at all. It is only quiet based on fear. How many invading armies have found out this truth to their dismay over the centuries? Gods' law? My understanding of Gods' law is that it must be based on love. Love must be the motivator and freedom of choice is the only way love can function. You cannot buy or force love.

Perhaps we are unsatisfied because we want to dictate the terms of our peaceful life. People would have to conform to my version of peace, order and good will to qualify for my heaven. Even Mother Nature would have to conform. Isn't it fortunate that I do not have such power? Perhaps even fortunate that God reserves this power to Itself?

What if we were to co-operate with nature rather than fight her? What if we were to learn how she works and go along? I think the reality, at present, is that we are at war with Nature. We expect her to bow to our demands. When she resists we have pollution, disease and famine. Does this not all arise from our foolish notion that we are special? Not only do we want to think that we are special

But we expect to be given special treatment by God. What a foolish and forlorn hope!

I now recognize that I am unique but not special. I am one with "All That Is" or God. There is no line where I stop and God starts. I realize that from knowing this to really learning to practice this truth, may be a long process or, it can happen in an instant of clarity. No one thing is special. All things are one thing.

I am open to this journey. I "practice the presence" and move slowly toward the goal of full unity in mind and thought.

My life is enriched, my hope is renewed and I look forward with joy to my progress.

I give thanks for this hope. I move forward with joy. I release this treatment to the Law of love and let it be so now and So It Is!

1. The Family of God William Gaither 1971.
2. Matthew 5:45.
3. James 2:1-9.
4. See A Course in Miracles, Foundation for Inner Peace 1975 Chapter 24 "The Goal of specialness."

Seven: Resurrection

Resurrection is one of the basic doctrines of most Christian religions. As it is usually presented, it says that at some time in the possibly distant future, all will be called to judgment. As a result of this judgment some will inherit bliss while others will be condemned to everlasting punishment. (bliss or blister) In any case the graves will be opened and the dead revived to stand judgment.

This makes resurrection one of the very distant things and therefore something that can be pushed to the back of the mind. The threat of damnation is often used as a scare tactic in an attempt to frighten folks into being "good."

However there is another way of looking at resurrection that makes it current and practical now.

Here I am using the #2 definition from Webster, "Resurgence or Revival."

When a person has "seen the light" and changed their life style from crime to service did they not have or experience a resurrection or a resurgence of life and hope?

When a person has been brought to a new understanding have they not experienced a resurrection in the here and now. People who recover from near death to live a normal life have experienced a resurgence. People who have "seen the light" and changed their life style from fear to love have experienced a resurgence or a resurrection. They have a new life NOW!

A big part of this resurrection experience is being able to let go of the past and forgive both themselves, and any other, for any real or imagined evil (harm) that they think they have caused, or that others have caused to them..

Many folks carry some sort of guilt burden on their conscience for a life time. In many cases there is no grounds for such guilt and they do not know how to release it. (This is called irrational guilt.) For others the guilt has a basis in fact. For both types the feeling of guilt is real. Do these folks not need a resurgence or renewal, a clearing of the slate? If they were to experience such a renewal would it not open up the possibility of new life?

In this sense, resurrection is a here and now event that it is possible for everyone to experience. It is one way in which God opens doors for us. It allows us to leave past wrongs, hurts and the burden of carrying them from the past into the future.

Would not such a resurrection of hope and renewal be a requirement for the healing of the rifts and feuds that exist among the nations? What hope has This world got if such an experience does not occur?

Interestingly enough, this resurrection experience is not limited to those who profess Jesus. It is a real experience for real people in the here and now. It comes to those who DO the work required. This work is internal work. It is based on re-evaluating re-organizing and re-ordering the life and thinking of the person. The "God Within" honours the work and so, in many ways it is a do it yourself project, although many will need help to get clear. For some it may come in a flash as they get new insights at a worship service. For others in a different way, perhaps at the work bench or in a dream. (Is it not sheer folly to expect that an "Infinite God" has only one way to get things done?) This is not to say that human kind can solve their own problems. We need and must have some Divine intervention to open our eyes. The light is in us without our awareness. 1 Only the Divine can open us to awareness.

Most of the guilt that people carry is self imposed and is irrational. You may hear of people who feel guilty because they were late getting to work and so missed the death so many experienced when the World Trade Towers were destroyed. This kind of guilt can only be released when the person carrying it can clear old and deep seated, false belief systems. Or when they have a spiritual

73

experience that turns them on to the true light. Jesus asked the question "when the light that is in you is darkness, how great is that darkness?" 2 Is irrational guilt not a dark light?

How dark must be our world if we are required to go back hundreds or even thousands of years to change, or correct, something that happened or was said to have happened to people who are long gone from the scene of action. When a person is forgiven and the slate wiped clean do they not have a new start? Is this new start not a form of resurrection right here and right now? How can the North American Indians, the Palestinians or any such group ever expect to get what they call justice for the real or imagined wrongs said to have been done to them hundreds or thousands of years ago? Only when we learn to leave the past, cease to lay blame and start to live in the now can we experience a true resurrection. We need to forgive any real or imagined wrongs done to us by the ancients, whether those ancients be white explorers or aboriginal peoples. This will open the way for renewal.

When we see nature coming back to life after a winter of sleep is this not a form of resurrection? Of course this experience is had only by those who live in the temperate or colder zones of our earth. When a person who has been severely injured and was unable to operate normally can return to a normal life style after healing, is this not also a form of resurrection? Might not this be a model that each person could take to heart in the here and now?

The Greek mythology had the Phoenix which could rise from the ashes of its own funeral pyre.

Is this not witnessed by the gardener who puts organic material (dead leaves etc.) into his garden and sees new growth spring from the old dead material he placed in the garden?

It appears to me that these principles are evident all around us. Only those who choose to complicate matters by removing them from the common experience can become confused and think they are "foolish airy fairy" religious notions. The God of reason and wisdom has ordered this system so that it re-cycles. The prophet Ezekiel speaks of "wheels within wheels." Are these cycles not wheels within wheels?

When we release the past with its' hurts and pain and begin to live in the now we open ourselves to resurrection and healing .

If we demand that God operate only within boundaries determined by our wisdom and always in some supernatural way, we blind ourselves to the truth. However if we choose to see God in every day things we can see how "IT" works through these principles on a daily basis.

The principle of resurrection is well established in nature for all to see.

I see no reason to think that the same principle does not extend into the unknown future where "man goes to his long home."3

We can observe that the universe re-cycles itself and so is not consumed into oblivion. By what logic should we assume that life is different from matter? Even if life was only a form of physical energy, (which I believe it is not) would it not still be reasonable to expect it to continue? Remember that matter can be changed to energy or energy to matter but it is not destroyed.

On the other hand if life flows from an Eternal Source (God) must it not also flow back to that source as water flows back to the sea?

You see life defies the normal process of gravity. Trees rise against gravity as does grass and animal life too. By some estimates the human body is over 66 % water. Now if you mixed water and mud in a proportion of 66 % water and 34 % soil or sand it would flow and by law seek its own level. It would flatten out. Wet cement has less that 66 % water and it flows until it dries. How is it then, that trees and humans both being composed of mostly water rise against gravity? Is it not due to the fact that Life has entered into the picture?

My contention is that Life Is Eternal. It is an intangible in one sense but it changes whatever form it inhabits. Life is very stubbornly determined to continue to exist. Just look at the trees clinging to a mountain side where virtually no soil exists. Or see the grass pushing through a concrete side walk Might it be possible that one guide to understanding God would be to say that "God is LIFE?" As such we have already noted that eternal life is Gods life. It can go through transitions but it does not go away.

Recycling may be a possibility but life continues. The only question in m75y mind would be if identity also continues. Most religions seem to teach that identity does indeed continue. This is held up as one of the reasons that we need to behave ourselves here and now. Some teach that a person might be recycled to return as a pig or a fly if they were too disgusting in their human form. Others say that judgment will take the form of punishment or even torture for the wayward person. However one looks at it most expect that life is eternal.

For this reason resurrection is not only a regeneration of life style in the here and now, but also an idea that reaches into the distant future. It follows along the line of the physical theory that matter can only be changed but not lost. So too, life can be changed in form but not lost and gone forever.

I am convinced that there is one source and one director of the processes that occur in my world. I call "IT" God and I am one with IT. Some of the thoughts and ideas I have are Divinely inspired. I sort through and need discernment to choose the positive and growth producing, those that are Divinely inspired.

I learn and grow by the same process as do the other creatures of nature. I learn here a little and there a little.

My progress is often marked by reverses and wrong turns. Yet I know that all these steps are possible steps to evolutionary growth.

My horizons expand. my world view expands and my life is enriched.

I give thanks for this increased knowledge of truth and with joy I now release this treatment to the Universe and let it be so. AND SO IT IS!

1. John 1:8-9.
2. Matthew 6:22-23.
3. Ecclesiastes 12:5.

Eight: Repentance

Repentance is not a very acceptable word to many. However Webster reports that one optional meaning is "to change your mind." I like to think of it as the attitude of being teachable. To be teachable is to change your mind or to open it to new things or ideas. In this sense all the advances in science are the result of persons being willing to open themselves to new or different ideas. In fact repentance (not penance) is nothing more that learning from our mistakes and doing things more wisely in the future.

Is the concept of our superiority not an idea that we need to review? Might it be wise to replace this old and failed idea with one of international brotherhood?

One biblical story in this area is the story of Ham. 1 Ham was cursed and marked for servant hood by his father (Noah) because he made fun of Noah's drunkenness. Another is the story of Hagar. 2 She was the mother of a bastard son by Abraham (when she was united in sex with Abraham without the benefit of marriage) and her son, Ishmael, could not be treated the same as Abraham's other son Isaac, who's mother was married to Abraham. 3 Perhaps by the choices of their parents, some children reap a harvest of dire consequences. Perhaps this is not Gods' desire but natural law and human prejudice at work. The reason that I bring these old tales up is that it shows the longstanding prejudice that some folks hold toward others. Whatever the circumstances of Ishmaels birth, surely they were not his doing and so another biblical contradiction occurs. "The sins of the fathers are not visited on the sons" or are they? The ten Commandments 4 say they are visited on the children while Ezekiel says they are not. 5 Was Ham or Ishmael of less value in the sight of the Divine than was Isaac or Hams brothers? Do these false concepts not arise from the human, limited, and thus sinful point of view? Are they not the result of our brokenness? Is our brokenness not the result of our basic sin? Do not our other sins, or most of them, rise from our faulty view of reality?

All too often those seeming sins are still charged to the children. Ham is considered the father of the black (servant?) races and bastard sons still have to fight from the position of the underdog. Our old prejudices die hard. Ishmael is considered Father of the Arabs.

In the West, or at least in Canada we are not taught about the exploits of the Chinese, the Hindus or the old ruins of a civilization found in Africa and attributed to the African people. (Information readily available now on the internet or any good encyclopaedia.) 6 With the exception of Egypt and the pyramids, very few westerners know anything about African civilizations. The result is that we often tend to think of these people as backward, lazy and stupid. This lack of information about others helps to sustain the barriers to brotherhood. Our schools do not teach about Chinese sailor/explorers, African inventions or other "Third World peoples. We are so focussed on our own importance that we ignore ideas that do not come from our accepted sources. These barriers are evident in our own cities and in the way many disrespect the beliefs and customs of others.

Do we all not need to repent and give a little, while taking (learning) a little from our neighbours? How long can the world tolerate foolishness like the Palestinian issues? These are traced back to Ishmael. Slavery in the U. S. was traced back to Ham. These old stories are still held up by some as "the word of GOD" and used to justify the old behaviour.

It seems to me that when the suggestion is made that God had something to do with a thing, some folks get totally unreasonable. It seems that their fear of God's retribution makes them crazy. 7 They become fanatical either for a literal interpretation of the text; or they want to totally disregard the whole thing. At that point they cannot or will not examine the issue on its merits. Either they hide in the "safety" of "it's in the book," or they toss the whole thing out.

I have a little reminder. It goes this way "It's not the things I don't know that get me into trouble. It's the things I DO know that just aint so!"

(Of course there is some comfort in being sure. Would this type of comfort not be short lived if the thing we were so sure of was not so?) Remember Jesus story of the house builder who built on sand. 8 Must this builder not have been sure that his foundation was secure to have built where he did? Might he not have called his friends and neighbors in to show off his new home? Yet when the storms came----. Might New Orleans be a modern example? Very often the people of science are far ahead of the religious. They are often open (but not always) to ideas different from and originating outside their own culture. Being open to new ideas is unnerving for some as it upsets their complacency.

The English bible is composed of the work of many persons and some are of doubtful integrity. King David could kill people on whim as he killed the messenger. 9 but he is still held in high esteem. All his wives and concubines did not harm his reputation.

While some of the biblical prophets attributed

national troubles to the peoples sin; this was also done by the enemies of Israel. Their prophets also saw the distress of their people caused by Israel as the judgments of God against them. 10 Might this suggest that God was not in favour of "sin" by any of "ITS" children? We are all; after all, children of earth and we come from and return to earth; at least in our physical elements. Surely Chief Seattle was correct when he observed that "we belong to the earth. Not the earth to us, and whatever happens to the earth happens to the children of earth." 11

While most recognize that we are all children of earth, those in privileged positions expect to maintain their advantage. This leads to the exploitation of the poor and as our "Global Village" grows smaller and smaller and more densely populated these differences become more and more evident to those who are exploited. This leads to a state of desperation among the poor. This desperation grows more and more acute until desperate people take desperate measures.

Surely only as we all, as God's children, wake up to this need and take steps (repent) to bring real change, can we expect to have peace. So in my opinion repentance is a necessary forerunner to peace. Otherwise we have at best, only the peace imposed by force of arms. Such armed peace is not peace at all, rather it is only quiet and that, only for now. Today even peace imposed by force of arms only leads to acts of terrorism. Some peace!

Repentance may also be applied to situations of pride. Is pride not the main stay of the argument that the privileged deserve their places? Are pride and ignorance not also the elements that block people from knowing each other as people rather than "Gentiles" or "Foreigners" or "Nips" or "Wops or whatever slur may be cast on those different from us?"

Repentance will also apply to those who place themselves at the top of the power structure. Is disregarding the Creative power of nature, God or Mother Earth not a cause for repentance? Does failure to recognize a Power greater than ourselves not indicate a need for repentance? If I recognize such a power must I not also become subservient to it? Of course then I would have to accept the fact that I was not the final arbiter of all things.

Repentance calls for a certain amount of humility. Only as we look with humility or an open mind can we see and recognize the roots of division and strife that raise plants of war and hatred. It will certainly require humility to admit our (yours and my) part in the mess and for us to be willing to make the needed changes. The first step in repentance is to acknowledge our part in creating

84

or maintaining "the manure pile." This principle applies to nations as well as individuals.

Is it not a form of repentance (as well as evolution) that brought us from the Model "T" Ford to the modern computer controlled autos of today? People found a better way and adopted it. Is that not the simplest form of repentance?

The image of someone crawling on their knees over broken glass is a very false and misleading concept of what repentance really is. This is more properly termed penance and has no place in my theology.

Some of these old images certainly need to be erased from our minds and replaced with more positive and productive ideas.

What we have here is an excellent example of the difference between religion and spirituality. Religion tends to encapsulate experiences and place rules around them. Thus you MUST or must NOT do so and so. These rules become rigid and the originators of the rules begin to have a vested interest in enforcing them. Hence "tradition" and "precedent" become the guides. These become a straight jacket and limit our chance for growth or progress. Spirituality, on the other hand, allows for freedom. How can we, or anyone else determine that there is no way but our way that God can reach out to "IT's" people? Would not an infinite

God have an infinite number of ways to approach us and an infinite number of ways for us to approach IT? The hazard with this kind of freedom (spirituality) is that some of these infinite ways lead to infinitely disastrous results. This would be one reason for the rules that govern religion. However I believe that the glory of God is intelligence and that we have been gifted with a measure of intelligence. Therefore we are capable of examining, testing and to some extent, at least, predicting the results of a course of action. Thus spiritual claims or experiences must be examined and tested. If they lead to evident disaster, we should be intelligent enough to reject them.

Do not forget that television, manned flight and many other technical advances were made because of visions that would have been and were considered pure madness by people of earlier times. Do we not block spiritual growth by our certainty that new ideas must be rejected? Is this not another reason that we need to practice repentance and allow ourselves to become teachable?

I know that repentance is a growth process. I know that forgiveness and freedom flow from repentance.

I know that it is presided over by the One power

that is in and through all. This Power I call God and I am one with it here and now. Therefore I am open to examining new ideas and testing them before adopting or rejecting them. I am willing to grow and change.

All I am is God but I am not all that God is.

God lives in me below the conscious level and I catch glimpses of IT from time to time.

I cultivate these glimpses and open myself to greater and greater visions. Always remembering to test the new insights for validity as best I can.

It is with joy and thanksgiving that I travel this road to understanding.

I joyfully release this treatment to the Universe and let it be so now. AND SO IT IS!

1. Genesis 9:18-27.
2. Gen 16, & 17: 18-22.
3. Gen. 21:8-20
4. Exodus 20:5
5. Ezekiel 18:1-20
6. See articles on Kush and Meroe as examples.
7. Revelation 22:13-15 is an example of the source of this fear.
8. Matthew 7:24-27.
9. 2 Samuel 1:1-16.
10. Gods Other Books P. 19   Elbert Dempsey Herald House
11. The Power of The Myth Joseph Campbell with Bill Moyers P.34. Double Day 1988.

Nine: Faith

Faith: According to Webster includes trust or belief. Try reading one of these other words, trust or belief into the text where faith is mentioned.

It is always interesting to me that some folks seem to fear anything to do with faith.

At the same time they jump into their cars and drive merrily along, exercising faith, unconsciously no doubt, but nevertheless placing faith in the other drivers ability to abide by the road rules. Many have ridden in airplanes and probably never once thought to question the amount of fuel on board or the competence of the flight crew.

We exercise faith when we cast our ballots in an election and when we send our children, for most people, their most precious treasures, off to school. While they might be able to check on the curriculum etc. most probably did not, thus it was unseen. Talk about faith.

However when asked to have faith in what they claim is unseen, it is a different matter entirely. Did they see the fuel level in the jet plane? Did they see the state of mind of the oncoming motorists? How many personally checked out the prescribed studies set out for their child or the state of mind of the teacher? They tend to be satisfied that they could check on these things if they wished. Because faith in God is not so easily checked out it is more easily dismissed as folly.

The fact is that we live in faith all the time. We have faith in the air worthiness of the planes we board even though we know that some do not arrive safely at the expected destination. We allow doctors to cut into our bodies. Is this not an act of faith or trust? We walk the streets and drive over bridges and in so many more ways display our faith on a daily basis. Some will say "prove that God exists or that the universe is not an accident." I think that by its very existence we are offered the proof. We believe in sounds that we can only hear with special equipment, light that only radios can "see" germs that are invisible to the naked eye. Perhaps we could "see" God if we had the proper equipment or perhaps only the correct frame of mind is needed. Perhaps we DO see God in one form (LIFE) and do not recognize it for what it is. (Even the rocks have a form of life as the sub-atomic particles within them dance and spin in an orderly manner. This dance seems to require some sense of awareness on the part of the particles.)

The fact is that we already know that faith is a part of our daily life. The thing that bothers many is not faith per se but Faith in an unseen Power that brings order out of chaos and that some folks have the temerity to claim a first hand knowledge of.

This becomes an abuse and is used by some so called religionists, or priests, as a lever to gain power in the name of God.

The big argument about the nature of God and the power struggle around this issue does cause many thinking folks to withdraw. The likelihood is that most of their claims regarding the understanding of the mind of God, and even the name or title are over stated. Are we not throwing out the baby with the bath water when we write the whole thing off for such reasons? Do farmers not exercise faith when they plant seed in the ground, at great expense, not knowing if this year may or may not bring a crop failure?

No doubt these farmers would argue that statistics will show that there is a very high percentage of years when good crops are grown. Motorist would argue that most trips end successfully and travelers, that most plane rides are safe.

I think that the laws of the universe require that success follows safe practices and again these laws DO imply a LAW GIVER do they not? The fact that we do not fully know these laws leaves us unable to predict with one hundred percent accuracy, every outcome.

Faith is evidently used and required; to live in the modern world. This faith is in "Tangible things."

We seem to have no trouble exercising faith in tangibles but great trouble doing the same for intangibles. We become stressed when asked to have faith in the "Intangible." Yet love and hope are both intangibles to my mind.

Have you ever seen the little test where a pattern is established but left incomplete and you are asked to indicate the next block in the sequence? It seems to me that this is all that is being asked of us now. The pattern of evolutionary progress, the evidence of an orderly universe where "laws" may be established that predict a sequence of events (from the weather patterns to the strength of steel). These patterns seem to me to be in sequence and my faith is nothing more that an affirmation that I can predict the next step.

If not predict, at least believe that this step may be taken safely.

Interestingly enough there are always options. These rise from our problem with freedom of choice. The next step in our world and in our evolutionary progress may be "back to the drawing board" or "onward and upward." It is our choice, a group choice. If we continue to allow fear and hatred to rule and dictate our choices, back to the drawing board is the most likely option. There is no rule however that says we cannot change course. This is what repentance is about. The old "myths" about Ham and Ishmael and people over thirty and blood making it better, need to be re-examined, evaluated and taken for what they are worth. In some cases they may not be worth much. Remember it was the "Hippies" who said "you can't trust anyone over thirty." Now that most of them are over thirty they are willing to forget (re-evaluate) their slogan of the past. Is not re-evaluation a form of repentance and faith too?

This form of repentance is the only way that we can ever take advantage of the learning that has been developed by people outside our little enclave. To refuse to look in other cultures and schools of thought is the height of arrogance in my view. To me it says that only me and my group have anything to offer. "My aren't we smart?"

In a very real sense, faith is the underlying principle that makes the others work. This regardless of whether the faith is placed in God, science or humans.

I am convinced that there is one mind and one source from which all things flow. I believe that I am one with that source which I call God. I open my mind to possibilities and my heart to hear. I release all ideas of superiority and specialness. I know that there is much that I do not see and much that I cannot see with my present physical equipment.

I know that God has new visions and new frontiers for me to visit and explore. I open myself to new ways of thinking, doing and seeing in the faith that the Divine within me can and will open my eyes and my understanding to the new and positive from time to time.

I give thanks for this assurance and I claim it now for myself.

I joyfully release this treatment to the Law of The Universe and let it to be so now. And So It Is.

Ten: Hope For the Future

The thought that our next evolutionary step might be "back to the drawing board" is offering a pretty bleak outlook for human kind.   What basis, if any do we have for hope?

However intangible hope may be, it is almost an absolute necessity for human life.   When hope is lost people give up.   When hope is lost they become desperate, commit ridiculous acts even suicide. What then, do we have as a basis for our hope?   For those who have no faith in an unseen God there may be very little hope.   Humankind seems to have demonstrated beyond any reasonable doubt that it is not only the most deadly animal in existence but also, as a species, the only one that is bent on "more" irrespective of the cost to our earth home, or to our other "co-residents" of earth.

An animal that goes on a killing spree is thought to be deranged (mad) and is destroyed. Yet over and over we go through war after war and all of them based either on "religious" issues or on greed. Greed may be for power. Even the religious issues often come down to lust for power which is a form of greed. I think that many religious leaders assume absolute power over their followers. Talk about unseating God! (not in reality of course but in imagination only.)

However, for those who do have a faith and do not

get so fanatical about it that they want to use force
to MAKE people comply with their version of
"religious truth" there may still be a glimmer of
hope that either we will eventually wake up to the
concept of UNIVERSAL BROTHERHOOD or
that God will intervene in some way to bring sanity
to an insane world. (Remember that Gods'
problem is, "ITs" gift to us, our right to freedom
of choice.)

Acts of kindness are experienced even among the
enemy soldiers in war and acts of self sacrifice and
charity are so common that they usually go
unmentioned and un-noticed in our news reports.

One of the problems with freedom, and God seems
to have decreed freedom to all "ITs" children. And
our freedom is infringed when another person or
nation attempts to force something, whether it be
good or bad in the eyes of the one doing the
forcing, on us. Our freedom is not honoured if we
are forced into anything. Freedom only works well
under conditions of mutual respect. That respect
allows both parties to exercise their freedom
without interference. In other words our freedom is
curtailed by the existence of another.

God must have the same problem. Either we are
free and can make our choices or we are not free
and at some time God will "whip us into line."

Personally I think that this idea of God resorting to

force is away off base. So my hope is that we will finally come to our collective senses and start acting like children of God. Acting as if we were brothers. Failure to come to this place may well take us back to the caves or even further back to some peculiar beast that can stand radiation..

This is not an irrational faith in my book. There is a sense of brotherhood taught in all world religions if people wanted to find it. The "Holy War" in its' best sense, is not designed to be against our brothers but rather it is an internal struggle to control the very ideas and impulses that now drive us to war. The monks who leave the world of action to live apart in a monastery and people who retreat are waging that war. It is a struggle for SELF CONTROL. The apostle Paul noted this war raging within himself as do other religions. [1] However, speaking for myself, I find it easier and more comfortable (in the short term) to blame and try to control others. Of course, in the long run no one can control another. I am the only one I can control. That control is self control.

We can gain self control when we stop listening to power crazed leaders who are green with envy for what others have or seem to have. It can be won when we start to use our own thinking apparatus and start to look beyond colour and creed to the Person within.

All people, except those who ARE crazy, want health and safety for their children. All bleed when cut and all "normal" people honour truth and personal integrity.

For me, hope is based on the possibility that sane people everywhere will come to realize these truths and refuse to follow "war mongering" leaders who would mislead them into power grabs that only seem to satisfy the ego of those leaders. What it really satisfies is their need to act as if they were God. And we, the people will foolishly continue to follow them as long as we think it pleases God for us to do so. No matter how much distortion we have to apply to the concept of a loving God in order to keep our old ways of thinking intact.

More and more people are becoming educated and are learning to think for themselves.

There is also the phenomenon of "critical mass." This seems to be a situation where, when a sufficient percentage of the group (human kind in this case) begin to act in a certain way and think in that way, a change takes place in the thinking and actions of the rest. According to this theory, when about two or three percent of the people start to really see all people as brothers and sisters the rest will shift their thinking in this direction also. This is not such a daunting task as would be getting one hundred percent of the population to change thinking. It is a doable project.

What we focus our attention on grows as that is where our energy is invested. Therefore if we focus on fear, war machines and "Star war" defence systems are the result: and we grow our fears and our enemies. Large defence budgets are required if we exploit our weaker neighbours, victimize them and cheat them. We treat them as "less than" ourselves. This becomes a ripe field into which radical hate mongers can introduce ideas of war and revenge. We arouse envy and hatred. They become angry and see no way out but war. The most powerful armies are no longer a defence against this tide. Modern war is not fought on the "field of honour." It is a war of terrorism. guerrilla actions and treachery by unknown and nameless people. Only a change of heart can alter the trend toward destruction. The "powerful" nations have enacted laws that protect their business interests. They have dispatched armies to protect those interests and used their own poor folks as "cannon fodder" in the interests of business. We need a grass roots movement to bring about change.

There are many people at this moment who are recognizing that the power is within themselves and that they are the creators of the life style that they experience. Anger, fear, war and peace are all choices that we choose to make. Once a sufficient group of people come to this realization and start to choose peace instead of war, anger and rivalry, we may well have the instrument needed to change the world in which we live. As A Course In Miracles says "I could see peace instead of this." 2 "I choose the feelings I experience." 3   In the meantime, we can take control of our own lives and experience more joy and success than we have been used to. This can become a demonstration of how things really can work.

I see life as a continuum and the course of The Divine is one eternal round. It is the power by which all things exist and move. I call "IT" God and I am one with IT here and now. I believe that this power is infinite, intelligent, conscious and active in my world. I believe that IT is working even now to raise my consciousness and that of all the human race to new levels of awareness and understanding. I sense a growing wave of human awareness that we are all one and must all live together or die together. We have the choice. I have   hope that wisdom and God will prevail to bring about the vision of unity and love which is the universal dream of humankind.
It is with joy and hope that I release this treatment to the Law and let it be so now.   And So It Is.

1. Romans 7:21-23
2. A. C. I. M.- Lesson 34
3. A. C. I. M The responsibility for sight. P. 418 1985
edition

Eleven: The Lords Prayer 1
(The Kingdom and relationships)

"Our Father who dwells in Heaven" (The human idea of utopia and the local god. Heaven, theoretically the place where God lives. Remember that we have already discussed where God lives.) Note also that it is phrased as "OUR" not "MY" Father. It recognizes a source beyond self. A source from which ALL people, nations and tongues and things flow. By implication this suggests a Fathers' concern for all his family. It is a social system.

"Hallowed be Thy name;" Perhaps a friendly and respectful relationship with God? The casual use of Gods' name in profane communications does not show respect for The Divine. Thus we are invited to Hallow or respect the name; and also the owner of that name. Words are creative and thus respectful words directed toward God might be more productive of peace than angry words. Might respect for the name applied to the creator not lead to respect for the creator ITSELF and for the creation? Is this not important if we recognize this power as our source? Perhaps it might even raise our level of respect for self and for others.

"Thy kingdom come, thy will be done on earth as it is in Heaven." We have great dreams of how heaven will be. Our dreams are based on our own prejudices and biases. They are not based on the ultimate truth that God must operate from. Don't forget that God is Father of ALL people. Might we need to be "colour blind" to find a place in Heaven? Or even in an earth where Gods will is done as in Heaven? Perhaps Heaven is a state of mind and not a geographic location. Is this prayer not a call for social justice and brotherhood among people of all races and colours? 2

"Give us this day our daily bread." This is still in the group mode. We are asked to pray for more than just me. We need no more at any time than for THIS Day. Money, power and immense stores of "stuff" only complicate our lives and these "reserves" begin to control our lives. They make other, not so fortunate folks feel envy and anger. We fear.

We must hire guards, build fences and lose sleep while we plan ways to out wit the supposed robbers that we will find to be both real and imagined. Note that this day is much longer than twenty four hours. 3 We must put into reserve the supplies needed for winter and even possible famine. However this proviso does not justify huge reserves being held at gun point while other human beings starve. It is noted that in the story of Joseph of Egypt the food reserves were shared with people who were not Egyptians. 4 Note also that nowhere in this prayer is there any request that our life be extended. Because God IS Life and life is eternal, death or transition is only a form not and end. There is no reason to fear death. When Jesus is quoted as saying "take no thought for tomorrow" I think in modern language it is much more useful. He is said to have advised "don't worry about tomorrow." 5 Worry is different from reasonable planning.

"Forgive us our trespasses as we forgive those who trespass against us." We are not expected to be flawless, only to know that we can be forgiven as we forgive. Remember that God is IN ALL. Therefore we cannot hide from "IT" and so when I harbour a grudge against my neighbour, God keeps it in front of me. This keeps me in turmoil and poisons my life. This is not a vindictive act by the Divine but simply an application of law.6

The question is do you live in a three or a four dimensional universe?

"3"D"universe	4 "D" universe
Width	Width
Length	Length
Height	Height
No time	Time

Past--------------------X----------------------Future.

NOW

*   Some of us live off the scale as in

the 3 d universe where the star is and where there is no time. In this place we have no power at all. Living in the past or the future is equally disempowering. Only in the NOW is power available to any one of us.

In the 3 "D" universe there is no time and nothing can exist. Or I live in an ever present now. In this case all hurts are current. The house you live in exists in time. It was not here in the days of Caesar. You: in your present physical form also exist in time. In the 3 "D" universe I do not separate events in time. Therefore I carry past events with me and act as if they were current. Thus I am always in pain and anger as I carry old hurts and old grudges with me. Therefore there is no forgiveness in me. If I live in the past I can accomplish nothing.

If I live in the future I am beset with worry and can accomplish nothing.

If I live in the NOW but recognize past and future I can learn from the past and plan for the future. If I am trapped in the past, or partially trapped in the past, I am stuck in that aspect of my life.

I am the only one who can choose to hold the grudge and also the only one who can decide to let it go. If I refuse to let it go it will poison my life. How I see time is a huge factor in determining my ability to forgive. If I live in the 3 d universe all past hurts are present with me now. I carry them nurse them and probably seek revenge. It is the grudge that poisons my life. Therefore I control and am responsible for how my life goes. While I am responsible for my choices etc., again the prayer is phrased in group terms. There are some trespasses against our group as there are trespasses against all other groups. These must require group forgiveness. In one sense groups act as lager persons.

"Lead us not into temptation but deliver us from evil." This does not make any sense to me. I believe that God does not tempt us ever. 7 Some translations render this phrase as "do not bring us to hard testing." 8 Or "do not cause us to be tempted." This makes better sense to me. We are asking that our trials of life be such that we can triumph over them. Notice the "WE" again. We are recognizing that there are forces in our world that we judge to be evil and we ask that we not fall into those situations. (Even if Evil is only in the eye of the beholder, we would not wish to be seen as doing evil or harm to another.)

If I have expectations that are not met; this may lead to evil. The bridge between expectations and reality is RESENTMENT. This resentment is against you if you do not live up to my expectations. The bridge between my expectations for myself and the reality is GUILT.

Thus my expectations of your performance leads me to resent you, if your performance falls short.

For me low Performance leads to GUILT if I fail to deliver as I expected of myself.

These two bridges between the real and the desired lead to the evil of blame against self and others. Is this not evil? In this sense we may do evil to ourselves as well as others.

I choose, as each of you chooses; the circumstances of our lives. We may do so inadvertently or by design. The choice may even be a consequence of group action. However we are praying that we not find ourselves in a situation that we would judge to be evil because of the consequences to us. May our eyes be open to the harm we can do inadvertently to self and to others. "For Thine is the Kingdom and the power and the glory for ever." We are putting God first. We are admitting that we are not in control. To really mean what we are asked to say here I must put God ahead of me. A relationship that is quite appropriate considering that God is "ALL IN ALL." Remember that we are cells in the Divine body so we are not being overlooked. We are not being asked to deny ourselves but only to put things in proper perspective. The world into which we are born is filled with enough and to spare. It is self sustaining and recycles automatically.

However when we violate our "Mother Earth" we upset that balance and skew the whole operation. The bottom line is that we have a relationship with our earthly home and when we disrupt that relationship even the earth becomes un-friendly. Our environment becomes polluted and the whole thing gets out of "whack." If we honour the "King" and the kingdom we also honour ourselves.

It seems to me that this relationship with our environment is basic. It is far more important to God and to us: than whether we call The Divine, God , Allah , Vishnu or Mother Nature. After all these are only titles employed by us in an attempt to describe or label that which is beyond us.

So many people have spoken of "Utopia, The millennium" or in some other way given voice to the dream of peace and brotherhood on earth. Is this not what The Lords prayer implies and what we ask for when we pray "Thy Kingdom come?" The Creator of all things must be expected to value all things. Therefore such an infinite power and possessing infinite wisdom would have a system whereby all things would, or could, work together for the benefit of all. Is not the statement "as it is in Heaven (or Utopia) so in earth, an affirmation of our notion that "all things work together for good" 9 in some place? Do we have any real idea of what

Heaven would be like? Or do we just assume that our ways are "right" and our standard of values ultimate? How far are we willing to go to accommodate ideas of others and the worth of other persons?

We are back to the coyote and the rabbit again. The coyote sees the rabbit as "good" and as lunch. The rabbit sees the coyote as "evil" and an enemy. However some people suggest that these two keep each other in balance and thus contribute to the balance of nature. The real question might be "what is the evil in this?" Might it be that evil is ONLY in the eye of the beholder?

Perhaps, if we could see the truly "BIG" picture, we would see that life is eternal and ALWAYS in transition. Maybe the time and place of our transition is not nearly as important as we tend to think it is. Maybe when Jesus taught us to pray "deliver us from evil" it was the concept of evil that he had in mind. After all if God is "in through and above all things." How can any of it be evil unless God is not as good as we think "IT" is? Might evil be nothing more than the dire consequences that we experience when we violate Divine Law? If in fact God is not good then we have; and this I refuse to believe, no hope. However most people seem to determine evil as that which does not satisfy their short term and short sighted goals. Good then is that which does meet these short term goals. This even if someone else is harmed in the process.

It is evident that the Lord expected us to have a sense of commonality and brotherhood. He incorporated this guidance into the words of his prayer.

I want to live in a world where I feel accepted., loved and to experience good health. Good health is three fold, Spiritual, mental and physical.

I believe that Spirit is eternal and yet it needs nourishment. However I believe that excellent mental health will nourish Spirit through awareness and cause the physical to conform as body is servant to mind.

My world must provide some challenge so that I can feel accomplished. This is basically the world in which I now live. I also want a world where brotherhood is the rule. The brotherhood of humankind is a choice. Brotherhood must be the rule and not the exception. A world where each is free and allows (respects) others in their freedom. Where we can all be free to follow the life path that each one chooses. After all, who has the right to demand my or any ones conformity. All I ask is that in choosing his or her own path they do not interfere with my path.

We each must allow the other the freedom to

choose and create the kind of life he or she desires. This requires that we stay aware of our surroundings and of how our actions are affecting our neighbourhood and our neighbours. I am free to swing my fists but must stop them short of my neighbours personal space.

I know that in the words of "The Lords' Prayer" Jesus gave voice to the hopes and dreams of humankind. I know that we are all one and one with the infinite Power that I call God. I now proclaim peace and brotherhood. I proclaim the oneness of all human kind. I also accept this proclamation as my own creed. I also realize that all things are a compound in one and so the reality is that we are all one. This includes the trees, the earth and all things in it. I choose to see God in all. I now release this proclamation to the universe knowing that my words have creative power. I allow this creative power to act to bring about the "Heavenly Kingdom" here on earth now.

I release this true statement to the Law and let it be so now. And So It Is!

1 . Matthew 6:9-14.
2. Isaiah 11:6-11.
3. Webster "Day a specified period of time as grandfather's day, an age----."
4. Genesis 42 chapter.
5. Matthew 6:25 New Century Bible.

6. Matthew 6:13-14.
7. James 1:13-14.
8. Mathew 6:13 Good News For Modern Man
9. Romans 8:28.

Twelve: "Truth?"

"YOU SHALL KNOW THE TRUTH AND THE TRUTH SHALL FREE YOU." 1

A famous question from the past is "What is truth?" 2

What indeed is truth or THEE truth? Probably only God ever knows THEE TRUTH. Among humankind the truth in the past was "the earth is flat." Current truth says that certain people are "evil" and certain others are "good." Yet some of the "good" people trample other Evil" people in their rush to amass great wealth and power. Their argument to justify such behaviour is either one of two, "business is business" or "these second class people do not deserve the good things of which we are worthy and for which we have worked so hard."   Of course this also presupposes that God has favourites.   In this line of reasoning the possibility that we are all Gods' children and that God might some day call people into account is discounted. However the question remains, are we all Gods' children and if so are we all equal before The Divine?   Wise earthly fathers do not play favourites with their children. However many of us are not wise enough to be completely even handed? Our anthropomorphic god follows our lead. Fortunately this god is imaginary. Some will assume that their business success is evidence of

112

Gods' favour. Might it not be possible that their business success is due to their practice of sound business practices? If the universe runs on principles would not observation of these principles result in success? Is this not how great buildings, automobiles and space ships are built? Would this not be true irrespective of the moral quality of the builders? Surely they are made using proven formulas that produce the desired results. However even partial truths may result in temporary success or at least limited success.

Another "truth" that is preached by some is that "our loving God" will condemn anyone who is not saved (by their standards) to "everlasting Hell." A place that they determine to be run by the devil and where one will "burn in the fires for ever." This god of theirs is so limited the he has only two choices "bliss or blister."

In this they overlook the opening message of Jesus "The Spirit of the Lord is upon me because he has anointed me to preach the gospel to the poor: he has sent me to heal the broken hearted and to preach deliverance to the captives--." 3 We find out from Peter that some of the captives were "disobedient in the days of Noah." 4 "Hell has enlarged herself and opened her mouth without measure." 5 "They will be gathered together as prisoners in the pit and be shut up in the prison and

113

after many days they shall be <u>visited</u>." 6 Ezekiel 32 identifies some who will be there and who the visitor will be. 7 "The strong among the mighty with they that help him" he says. We find out that the strong one is "the Lord" 8 Jesus also spoke of this. 9 and Peter makes it clear that "the gospel was preached to them that ARE dead" 10 Jesus even says that he has the keys to death and hell. 11 Why does he have them if not to release the prisoners? It seems clear to me that the INFINITE and Omnipotent GOD has unlimited options and does not play favourites according to the whims of those who claim to preach on (His?) "IT'S" behalf. only the anthropomorphic god invented in the limited minds of people is so biased and limited.

Here we have outlined only a few of the "truths" that float around this world. Is it possible that most people think that their way is the "right" way and thus the truth? Do I, or you or our group have the final say on what is right and true?

In fact, truth is one of the most abused words in our language. As was pointed out earlier, the rabbit sees the coyote as evil and dangerous. This is the truth to the rabbit. The coyote sees the rabbit as good because it represents lunch to him. This is the truth to the coyote. Only if the rabbit escapes is he seen as evil by the coyote.

Undoubtedly a great deal of our values for

determining good and bad are equally self serving. The saying "what is good for General Motors is good for us" is not always true. How much profit did they and other manufacturers like them, make out of the wars and out of the arms trade? How many lives would have been saved if they had pursued life and freedom rather that profit? Is not this same policy followed by many of us on a lesser scale? At the same time it must be

acknowledged that G. M. or many of the others did not create the wars. Nevertheless our military industrial complex has no incentive to change the system to make war obsolete. War provides employment and profit to some. True we must all provide as best we can for our loved ones but can we justify so doing when other folks are made the losers in the process? Perhaps the profit motive and competition is not the most "Christian" method after all.

All people see the world from their own point of view. This point of view is coloured by their cultural beliefs, their version of truth, the beliefs that were instilled in them by their culture and religion and by their attitude toward neighbours of same and different skin colour. In effect we see the world through our own window. This window has a four sided frame and each side projects a coloured glass across the window itself.

Our BELIEF SYSTEM is perhaps topmost in this colouring system. Whatever these beliefs are, spiritual, based on Nature or something else is of no consequence. What we believe is what we believe. First everyone knows that their religious beliefs are "true." Remember that we define religious beliefs in this context as "the belief system on which we run our lives." This whether God is included or not. (After all these "truths" were drilled into each one of us when we were defenceless or unable to make informed decisions. These were the truths that our parents and other authority figures held and passed on to us in our infancy. They also were the "word of God." If not the word of God, then at least the law as those in power made it; and so true for us. Anything that differs from this version of "truth" is automatically false and untrue to the mind of a child.) We tend to accept these "truths" and many of them are incorporated into our thinking un-examined. They are part of the culture that we just accept. Coming to understand this becomes one of the great needs of our time. We must come to realize that childhood ideas MUST be examined in adulthood and in the light of issues of brotherhood. When I speak of religious beliefs in this sense I am including as religious, any form of belief system that one holds. This would include the belief that

116

there is no God and that life is really "every man for himself." After all religion is what we believe and what we do about that which we believe. Thus only the nature of your god differs from person to person. Some worship money, some power and some self while others look for a source and an object or being worthy of worship. What we believe is what we believe. Our actions will demonstrate our beliefs no matter what we say. As Mark Twain said "your actions are making so much noise that I cannot hear what you are saying."

Our version of TRUTH is the second side of the frame. It casts a different colour across our window. The recognition that we do not KNOW the truth would clear up most of this colouring. Our OPINIONS are the third side of the window. Our opinions are closely related to our version of truth. However we hold opinions even knowing that they are not or may not be the truth. Our ATTITUDE is the fourth side of the window frame. Some folks do have an attitude that is described in the phrase "do not confuse me with facts, my mind is made up." In psychiatry this is described as denial. Most of us live part time in denial. It may also be summed up in the adage "I would rather be right than happy." Because of

117

these coloured panes of glass, when we look out of our window at our world our view is distorted and skewed.

As we look through our own window we have perceptions. On the basis of these perceptions we make decisions. These decisions lead to actions and these actions get us our results. It is important to note here that nothing has any meaning except the meaning that WE GIVE IT. 12 Since we have no idea what any given event or action means to God we decide for ourselves what it means to us. This is ALWAYS true.   Looking at my world and my life I am driven to conclude that my decisions were faulty at some point or points.   How about you?

Would it not be great if, even only for a second, we were able to see the truly "big picture" and know the real truth? How might the world be changed if for even a moment we could see clearly? 13 (Elishas' servant had such an experience. It is what A. C. I. M. calls "the Holy Instant?". 14

I do not think that such a possibility is likely to occur in the near future. However the mixing of the races and the mixing of the religious beliefs of the masses has possibilities for bringing human kind to the realization that we all want the best for our children.   We all bleed when injured and we all have feelings, hopes and dreams of peace and harmony.

Might we have happier lives if even this little fragment of truth was incorporated into our thinking?

I know that people have a universal need to find something greater than self to worship. While there are exceptions nevertheless people need to worship. Some worship beauty and some power. Some may even worship truth but through our coloured glass we are misled as to what the truth is. In realizing this fact, might we become more open to other folks and the ideas and experience of others? <u>We must remember that only God knows the real truth.</u>

I know that for many worship is taught and learned as a child. This form of worship is often thought of as childish and left behind when we become adults. I now open my mind to the truth of a power greater than me and worthy of my intelligent worship. I call this power God and I am one with it. It is in all things around all things and above all things. I am included in all things. It is truly LIFE. As I open my eyes, ears and my mind I have a hint of the Divine voice urging me forward into a life of joy and freedom. I have a vision of possibilities for the future. I examine my old and long held beliefs testing by logic, reason and also by faith.

My world opens up before me. I catch the vision of a bright future. I notice that I have a part in creating that future. I claim my place and I move forward with hope and joy into the bright unknown.

I release this treatment to the universe now and let it be so AND SO IT IS.

1. John 8:32.
2. John 18:38.
3. Luke 4:18 and Isaiah 61:1-2.
4. 1 Peter 3:18-21.
5. Isaiah 5:14.
6. Isaiah 24:21-22.
7. Ezekiel 32: all ; note 21-22.
8. Psalms 24:8.
9. Mat. 12:22-30, note 29.
10. 1 Peter 4:6..
11. Revelations 1:18
12. See A Course In Miracles Pub. by   Foundation For Inner peace 1985   Lesson # 1.
13. 2 Kings 6:8-17.
14. Chapter 15 A Course In Miracles.

Thirteen: Gods' Kingdom

If all the foregoing is even close to the truth does God have a plan or is IT just "muddling along?"

If there was no plan why would God have bothered in the first place? If there was no plan how did the earth become so astute as to be able to re-cycle and reuse virtually every scrap of stuff so that it continues as some say about the "eternal round" of the Divine?   If there was no plan what has evolution to accomplish?

I think there is a plan. A plan that calls for the co-operation of all the creatures of earth so that peace and harmony might prevail. A plan that may well open up doors to new and un-imagined possibilities for all human kind and for the earth itself. We are all reported to have a common ancestry. Does this not indicate a common need? It seems to me that we are in the process of moving either toward or away from that goal every day of our lives. It is an accepted fact that nothing ever stands still. If God is as stated earlier, in all things; then in fact; there is only one thing: GOD. It is only our blindness that keeps us thinking and acting separately. Remember, when Jesus prayed "Father forgive them for they know not what they do" 1 it was suggested that what they did to him they did to themselves. In another place Jesus said "in as much as you have done it to one of the least

of these my brothers, you have done it to me." 2
Jesus recognized that there was only one. If you
read the 17th chapter of John with this thought in
mind you will see this truth. If you and I could see
God in each other and all others what a change
we'd see.

Is there any good reason why we cannot be
constantly moving forward toward this goal of
brotherhood and peace?

Personally I doubt that there is any good reason for
failure to move ahead. However there are many
poor reasons for that failure. I think the plan calls
for our conscious co-operation in its progress. I
think that as long as we make foolish differences
and split hairs over minutiae the whole universe
waits and will continue to wait in vain. At present,
human kind is so blind and opinionated that it
refuses to see the same thread of life (the Divine)
in all things. We do not see the "oneness" of all
things. Thus we do not, or choose not to see that
what we do to the earth we do to ourselves. What
we do to each other we do to ourselves. It just
takes time for our actions to return to us. No one
of us is truly independent of the rest of us. Truly
we are interdependent because we really are one.
Only our awareness is lacking. This all stems from
our basic sin of seeing ourselves as separate and
each "other," and God as rivals. It is fertilized by

our notion that God is local and like us. Thus disharmony and distrust are rampant. These lead to fear, hate and war. War will not settle anything but only postpone the arrival of the Divine Kingdom on earth. A kingdom which is only a seed at present and a seed looking for fertile ground in which to grow.

True we can say the whole thing even now is the Divine Kingdom and we would be right. However this part of the Kingdom has the potential to be so much more than we now experience. The possibility of more seems to be built into the human psyche. Might God have built this into our being for good reason? It does not require much imagination to conceive of a more humane and friendly experience of life than so many now experience.

Is it possible that God is still working? The Genesis myth tells us that "he" completed the heavens and earth and rested. Does this mean the rest was forever? Jesus says that "My Father keeps working so I keep working too." 3 I note that there is nothing in these words of Jesus to suggest that God takes a day off.) It seems obvious to me that Gods' Kingdom is a process. It is even now in process and an INFINITE creator will NEVER run out of work. Perhaps our need for "more" is instilled in us by God. (Perhaps only the direction that we choose is in error. The major buildings of our day take years to complete. Might not Gods' Kingdom take an eternity to build to completion? Are we not talking of Gods' Kingdom when we dream of a world at peace?

A Course In Miracles says that the Genesis story reports that Adam went to sleep. However it points out that this story does not say Adam ever woke up. 4 I think we are still sleeping. We sleep in our un-awareness of The Divine. We sleep in our blind rush to gain power or what ever, apparently not realizing that we leave it all in a short time anyway. We sleep in our stubborn refusal to see that God IS in all and in each other. No wonder the "Kingdom" waits. No wonder it remain a dream. According to the Genesis myth God put us out of the garden. It does not say that God separated ITSELF from us however. Quite the contrary. God will never leave us. 5 Nevertheless separation is our explanation of why we do not see God in all. This is a "passing the buck" ploy to get us off the hook.

The dream as held in some form by almost all cultures may be called "Utopia" "Zion" or "the millennium" or even the "brotherhood of man." What ever it is called it is one of the reasons to hold on to hope.

I claim this hope and I hold this vision. Together

we can "make is so," in the words of
Jon Luc Piccard of the Star ship Enterprise.

I now see the unity of all things. I see God is all
and know that I am one with the all.
I open my eyes, my mind and my understanding to
see and learn. I deny the power of ancient tradition
to block my growth in the days ahead.
I am thrilled at the possibilities that open before
me. I joyfully enter in to this new world and
embrace the future with real hope. I now release
this hope to the Universe and let it be so. And So
It Is!

1. Luke 23:27-34.
2. Mathew 25:40 & 45.
3. John 5:16-17
4. A course In Miracles Chapter 2 The origins of separation.
5. Hebrews 13:5.

Fourteen: WHAT WE CAN DO

Since it is a fact that we can only control ourselves, change MUST start with each individual person.

Examine your own beliefs and those things that you hold as fact. See what portion is based on prejudice and ideas that divide. This is very hard work. It will require that a person make many changes in their thinking and in their actions. It will totally upset our smug superiority and open the way for real change. Remember that before change can have place, upheaval must occur. Old beliefs that were familiar, comfortable and reassuring must give way to greater light and understanding. Remember that Jesus said the condemnation was "that light has come into the world and men love (prefer) darkness." 1

The real truth of this situation is that many if not most of our beliefs are acquired from our environment. We pick up ideas, beliefs and attitudes from our environment. Our peers, parents, authority figures and local plus national traditions all contribute. Remember that small children are not yet equipped to screen incoming data. It is perceived by these little ones as the truth. Some of this information is so deeply ingrained that as adults we accept it without a second thought.

Those of us who are now adult can examine our

126

beliefs systems and test the validity of them in the light of logic, common sense and experience. However, even adults can fall victim to false ideas propounded by those seeming to be in authority. Think how Hitler sold a whole, highly industrialized and educated nation on the ideas of their superiority. This was called propaganda and led to World War two. This "super race" theory became the religion of the German nation during this period. Some aspects of our own religious belief systems may be equally fouled. The Israelites thought of themselves as "Gods' favourites." They saw all other as "gentiles" and as of less worth to God. Many "Christians" see themselves as having an "in" with God and non Christians as being "less than." Thus the need for self examination. Self examination sounds great but for most folks some sort of guidance or coaching will be required. When we see the contradictions in our own religion we can begin to open up to new ideas. Once we are clear on our own beliefs we can begin to change the environment in which our children are raised. If we teach them that God is a God of love: then must not this loving God love and reach out to all "ITs" creation? How might this affect our attitude toward gays, prostitutes or even those of a different main line faith or religion such as Islam?

We can teach our children to think and not to believe the first ideas presented.

Ideas of prejudice based on the superiority of the "white" explorers whether it was in the Americas, the Indies or Africa was a perception of the explorers and of the priests that traveled with them. It was based on a very cursory examination of the limited facts known to the newcomers. The priests were sure of their position as they could cite the biblical passages previously mentioned here and others as well. (Of course these biblical passages were infallible and they "knew" how to interpret them.) The curse of blackness and servant hood was easily seen in the dark people. 2 How could these folks be anything but servants. The bible gave the white man permission to so determine. This perception was carried to the children and the peoples of Europe. "Savages" were even brought back and treated like animals in the zoo as evidence of the European superiority.

Since it seems always to be the nature of people to like to think of themselves as superior, the idea was not hard to promote among the masses of Europe. Remember, that they, sub-consciously, thought that they were at the centre of the world and thus qualified to decide. They were "resident managers of the universe." It is quite common to find that people choose to hear what they want to hear. Many also ignore those things they do not like to hear. This is called "denial," or some might call it "selective hearing."

Think about how most people react to persons of a different religion. While some are open minded and will listen with care and attention many will discount the ideas and not hear at all.

A modern example of this kind of thinking was seen in the first professional hockey series between the Russian and Canadian best. The Canadian commentators were sure that the Canadians were superior because the Russian players had skates considered old fashioned in Canada. This to the commentators was evidence of Canadian superiority. The Canadians won the series on a lucky goal in the eighth game. A very simple example of the way folks tend to think that they are the best. Another example, not so funny was seen at the beginning of WW 2 when the commentators were bragging that the German army was in for trouble since France had the best army and Britain had the best navy in the world and the best air force. Hitlers' forces were outclassed from the start according to this theory. History shows that the German military were the best on all counts at the start and it took almost five years to wear them down and defeat them.

Also the "Allies" out numbered the German

populace. About three to one or even higher.

Just a little humility and some careful examining of the true facts would allow us to see that all humans bleed when injured, all are willing to give their lives for their children and all want to live in peace. This is true except for a very few who are sociopathic.

If these simple ideas were properly taught in our schools and by enlightened parents, the prejudices of the past could almost disappear in one generation. Of course there would always be a few diehards who would cling to the "old ways." Some would even make it a matter of religious belief saying "we are leaving the old and TRUE ways. The ways of God. God will be angry about this and you will pay." This calls on us to "fear" God. Such a God may be feared but it is not worthy of respect. Personally I think that respect is a much more appropriate choice of word in to-days language. God does not "fly into rages" as some would have us believe. A god that blocks progress and flies into rages is not worthy of respect anyway. In any event the "old ways" have not produced the Divine Kingdom on earth. Their legacy is war famine and distress. How much worse could the "new ways" be?

Another area of trouble is our conception of God, if we have belief in such a being. Is your mental picture of God large enough to meet the needs of the modern world? If your concept is of the "anthropomorphic" god. This being will play favourites as the ancient Israelites believed. They thought they had an inside track with God. Note that in most of the wars of modern time both sides call on God and claim the Divine blessing for their enterprise. In the most recent wars God has been invoked by different names. It is as if one had to get the name correct or the power of the universe would not know or respond to the entreaties of human kind. Of course each one "knew" that they had the inside track and had the name correct. It is as if our corner of the world is the only one that The Divine has interest or concern for. Following this foolish logic, if we win we are vindicated in our belief. However if we loose we find a different reason for the defeat. The usual reason given is usually a guilt trip put on people by their religious leaders, "your disobedience has angered God and so God does not listen." Thus God is exonerated from any charge of negligence in the loss. 3 Perhaps the whole idea of God must be re-evaluated. The "God" of the Old Testament was and is NOT worthy of the worship and blind obedience some pay to "him." The picture of God sketched in these and other scriptures is fragmentary at best. What we need is to free ourselves from these ancient and limiting notions. We need to open ourselves to examine the best of these and combine that with the newest insights. "Here a little and there a little" needs to be our guide.4

These ideas are not as far fetched as some may think. Peace, good will and brotherhood are terms that come up everywhere. They can only have meaning in our lives when we put them into action

I am convinced that there is one race of persons, the human race. One source from which we all sprang. I call this source God and I believe IT is within all. I will not see this if I only look outside for my information. The inner voice whispers to me and sometimes even shouts to be heard. I open myself to this source of enlightenment. I deny the old traditions and superstitions the power to prevent me from entering into this new world of oneness and light. I am blessed, enriched in spirit and challenged.

It is with joy that I open myself to this new understanding. It is with great expectations that I now release this affirmation to the Universe and let it be so.

And So It Is!

1. John 3:19.

2. Genesis 9:24-27.
3..2 Kings 17:7-18.
4. Isaiah 27:9-13.

Fifteen: Commonalities

It seems to me that any reasonable God would not pick out only one of IT's children to favour above all others. Therefore I must believe that God has spoken to many different peoples at one time or another: not just to Israel, Buddha or Mohamed. God must have spoken to prophets in ALL cultures at some time and to the extent that they could receive the message. 1 We must also know that because the message was and is transferred to people of limited understanding. It would become garbled with time. No doubt for the same reason it was already polluted to some degree by the first messenger to receive and bring it forward.

In this light we can look at the messages from all the great teachers and expect to find salient points of agreement. For example Mahatma Ghandi taught peace, as did Martin Luther King and the angels that proclaimed the birth of Jesus and Jesus himself. 2

The Bible says that "God is merciful." The Koran also says this but teaches, as does the Bible that "God has blinded their eyes." 3 What kind of love would blind their eyes and then punish them for their blindness? Yet some versions of the Bible imply that "they" blinded their own eyes because THEY (choose to) "walk in darkness." 4 There is another evidence of pollution as The Bible also states that God Is love. Yet it also teaches "an eye for an eye." 5 The Koran also calls for cutting off the hand of a thief, 6 yet almost every chapter opens with "praises to Allah the merciful and compassionate." Even when It teaches that "God has cursed the infidels, and has got ready for them ,the flame." 7 The bible also teaches that God is merciful. 8 The bible says that "The Lord our God is one God,"9 as does the Koran. 10 Bahi Say, "The earth is one country and humankind are its citizens."11

Nearly all religions teach some form of life after the end of this earthly life. Some even sent attendants and food with their leaders who were being buried, a strong indication that they believed in something beyond the grave. To phrase it differently all teach that there is more to life than we now see. They also teach moral values, although these differ depending on the group.

It has been said that God reached out to all. The bible says that when we are children we must be treated as children and fed milk. The problem for us is that each of us thinks that we are mature and can handle the "meat,"12 or that we are mature and understand. This must become a problem for God. However Jesus called his disciples "little children" 13 We know that we teach our children very simple versions of complicated matters.

More complicated versions are taught in university. Can God do otherwise? Anyone who remembers Aurthur Godfrys' "Ask The Children" T. V. show will remember how they went into flights of fancy to fill in the blanks in areas like sex, life and death and so on. Or think of how even seasoned reporters ask foolish questions when caught off guard by an emergency where they have not had time to research the issues. Does it not seem likely that we do the same to God? To say that God would intervene to prevent such events from happening is a childish dream. It would remove our freedom.

Another area of similarity is Karma. Karma is a Hindu idea. It promotes the concept of cause and effect. It states that life is not determined by fate. Rather we have free choice and there are consequences attached to our choices. Some of these consequences will be felt in this life. Some will be experienced in the next life. Since they believe in re-incarnation that next life will be experienced here on earth. In biblical terms "what you sew is what you will reap.[14] Or in Christian terms there will be a day of judgment at the time of our resurrection to a new life. Previous actions will affect our new state. In Hindu thinking God has a hand in this as do Christians. Buddhists and Janes also believe in Karma but tend to say that the consequences are a natural result of choice. They say God does not need to enter into the equation other than in setting up the natural laws. Karma was first taught by the Hindus and was later modified to suit the other two religions that teach it. In general they think that your karma can be discharged by proper acts; a form of repentance no doubt. Even in our justice system we often make allowances for good behaviour. It may be considered a mitigating circumstance in sentencing or for parole. Many Christians seem to believe in a God who has only two choices; Heaven or Hell bliss or blister. However Paul does not see it that way. "There is one glory for the sun another for the moon and another for the stars and as one star differs from another in glory so also is the resurrection." 15 It seems obvious that there is common ground in the concept of reward and punishment. The arguments arise when the where and how of these punishments is discussed. As in so many other situations "the devil is in the details" and who knows anything about the details. Who has reported on the facts. Jesus gave no details. He only spoke of a joyful and happy place; Abraham's Bosom" he called it. 16

It seems pretty clear to me that these people all saw some part of the same " Elephant" but not all, and like the blind men, they are sure they KNOW.

The North American natives also believed in life after death.

In the parable of the sheep and the goats Jesus seems to be teaching some form of consequences for the choices of those gathered before the judge.17 He also expects them to be aware and some to have an unhappy experience as a result of their choices. Is this not a version of karma? Might he also be teaching that we are all one; that what we do to another we do to ourselves? He is quoted as saying "if you did not do it to these my brothers you did not do it to me."

Arguments existed between the Sadducees and the Pharisees about whether there is life after death. This argument; in a different form shows up in Eastern religions too. Some say you pass into nothingness or Nirvana although some think Nirvana is a blissful state. Some teach about a "Heavenly hierarchy with God at the top and all sorts of angels, saints and other messengers in between. Christians, in general, teach that Jesus opened the way directly to God. Even so they speak of angels and other messengers. Some Christian people think that the "Saints" are intermediaries between God and the rest of us. Thus many of us have concepts that approach the pantheon of the Greeks or Norse. Even the ancient Greeks had a "Chief" god among their pantheon.

"HIS" name was Zeus The Norse, likewise had a chief god whose name was Odin. When we allow the saints, holy men and other messengers to come between God and man, have not most Western religions done the same thing? Our pantheon is different but still a pantheon.

You see, it is not the similarities that are looked at. Because each one claims to be RIGHT and to KNOW, they make fun of the rest. Any detail that varies from "MY" idea is WRONG and merits being mocked. Just like the blind men who went to see the elephant.18 "Each of them is partly right yet each of them is wrong." You can find most of these same arguments among the different sects in any major religion. Is it not time that we began to respect each other and compare notes with a view to finding common ground?

Consider the Pyramid of life. At its base is the mineral kingdom where movement is so slow that thousands of years are required for humans to see any change. Yet the sub-atomic particles move in an orderly way and dance at great speeds; for them: within the rocks of that kingdom. Built on the mineral kingdom is the vegetable kingdom where movement is much quicker. We can watch the plants grow and some will turn to the light.

Yet the vegetable kingdom could not exist without the older mineral kingdom. At the upper level we have the animal kingdom which can only exist based upon the vegetable.

Before we take this any further we need to point out that the vegetable kingdom could not exist were it not for the soil bacteria. Are not these bacteria a form of animal life? If so we have another circle where it is hard to tell the beginning from the end; "Alpha and Omega" both ends of the circle or first cause: God!.

When we examine the animal kingdom we find movement speeds vastly increased, awareness is very evident and some limited freedom of choice is expressed. However, only at the apex of the animal kingdom; i. e. among human kind is true freedom to be found. Humans are aware of their awareness and thus able (and required) to make choices on a conscious level. The evolutionary process could be directed by LIFE or God, up to this point. It seems that now humans must co-operate with "God or Life" if the process is to go any further. This is obviously an issue related to our freedom of choice. Many religionists refuse to see evolution in action here. Somehow they find it cramps their mental picture of God sitting on "his" throne. This picture of God is based on the picture of Nebuchadnezzar who required his subjects to bow and worship his image when called to do so.19 Does Islam not still follow that pattern

140

toward Allah? We have the same picture in revelations. 20   In any event religionist look back and so walk backwards into the future.

If God or First Cause or "Life" did, in fact move to communicate with the ancient people through the "prophets," what stops "IT" from continuing to do so?   The likelihood is that IT still does but blind and wilful religious leaders do not see it because of their backward stance. We have the command of Jesus 21 and the "Ten Commandments to name only two. These are clearly opposed to killing of humans. These requirements are written into our national laws yet "Thou shalt not kill" is totally ignored over and over, with government approval in war. Perhaps twenty million in World War One and another fifty million in World War Two and millions since in lesser wars and massacres. Might God have communicated these rules to people in the past? If so has God changed or do we just ignore IT's wishes when it suits our fancy?

Might it be possible that God does reach out even today? Might people like Wayne Dyer, Deepack Chopra, Mahatma Ghandi, Martin Luther King, Neale Donald Walsch,   Ernest Holmes and Barbara Marx Hubbard to name a few, be the prophets of the current age? And what of other sources such as "A Course In Miracles" 22 and "The Nature of Personal Reality" 23 that come

141

seemingly across the divide between life as we know it and life on the other side. Is this not how at least some of the biblical prophets claimed to receive their stuff? 24

It is to be noted here that the bible seems to allow for such communications. "Here a little and there a little--with a stammering tongue" --and "Now we see in part-."25

Should we not at least examine what these modern teachers (prophets) have to say before we choose to disregard them?

The other thing to note is that we, in the West usually are careful to keep our homes clean and in good condition. I think this is a universal desire where it is possible. However we as a race do not keep our "little space ship Earth" in good condition. 26 We seem to think that we can rape it and plunder it and do so with impunity. We have burned a hole in the O-zone polluted the north, poisoned the air in our major cities and even threatened the ocean. 27 We have also been the cause of the extinction of many species of animal life. Are we taking care of our home?

Remember the Jane and Buddhist conception of Karma; consequences follow naturally from our chosen actions so they say. They also teach that changing the behaviour can lift the karma. Is the present state of our home not the consequence of poor, albeit ignorant choices? How far can we push "Mother Earth" before she decides to get rid of us? We are told, according to the Genesis myth to "dress and keep" the garden. <u>26</u>   It also says to "have dominion over it." <u>28</u>   Does dominion give us the right to destroy it?

The fact is that we, the human race, live on a little "space ship we call EARTH. It has been given to us and it is self sustaining. WE have divided it into three decks. On deck one is the "First World." On deck two we have the "Second World" or those who are as technically advanced as the first world but who disagree with "First World" ideas. Then we have the "Third World" who are not technically advanced and therefore considered less than the others. However, some on deck three may be more humane than those above realize as they only look at deck three to mock and point to the faults. We put up barriers to prevent free movement between decks. Those on deck one have even jammed some of our "First Nations"(Third World people) into reserves and kept them there for generations.

The Captain of this ship seems to be invisible or absent so mutiny is rampant. This even though the Captain has left instructions. <u>29</u>   The problem seems to be that people have developed "legal minds" and can find ways to split hairs over what the instructions mean. Some even ignore the principles (listed in next chapter) and try to impose their ideas by force. In the attempt to establish their control they have blasted a hole in the ship, killed many of the crew and "lorded it" over those they have subdued. Obviously failing to note another principle, that people are free and this freedom is not compromised under any circumstance. Thus those who are subdued are plotting and waiting for their chance to get even. Getting even, of course defies another principle: that of forgiveness.

Those on decks 1 & 2 have weapons of mass destruction with which they hope to keep deck 3 in a subservient role. They have enough of these to destroy spaceship earth many times over. However some of those on deck 3 are close to, or have made small weapons of mass destruction of their own. In this mutiny and civil war on board Space Ship Earth much of the self sustaining quality of the ship itself is threatened. However the crew seems to be so angry and intent on getting their own way, on each deck and planning to control the other decks that they do not seem to care if the ship is destroyed.

Space ship Earth is in big trouble. Is there no one on board who can and will take the lead in settling their problems before the ship is destroyed?

I am convinced that there is one source, one power that is in and through all things. It is in me. I call "IT" God and I am one with it now. It operates the world in a manner that is self sustaining and governed by natural law. Intelligence flows from IT to all things and LIFE is IN IT. As I open my mind and my heart to see, my spiritual eyes are opened to this truth. I deny the power of cynical scepticism and cold Godless logic to deflect me from this path to enlightenment. I see the circle of life and the endless nature of my being.

My life is freed from fear, hate and envy. I move forward in love and I see the face of God in each person that I meet. I have respect and love for all. I see hope and joy in the future as people come to this understanding.

It is with joy and thanksgiving that I claim these truths and I release this treatment to the Universe now and let it be so. And So It Is!

1. Book of Mormon   2 Nephi 12:60-65   Community of Christ version.
2. Luke 2:8-10. & Matthew 26:50-52.
3. John 12:38-40 & Koran Sura 2 :6
4. 1 John 2:11. John 12:40 Lamsa translation and Isaiah 6:9-10 ibid. John 3:17-20. Koran Sura 2:10 Ivy books '93
5. Exodus 21:4
6. Koran Sura 5:42 The Table. Ivy Books Translated by J. M.   Rodwell   1993.
7. Sura 33:64

145

9. Deuteronomy 6:4

10.   Sura 3: 1 and others Sura 5: 77-80   Ivy Books   by Ballantine 1993 edition.

11. A Bahi principle

12. 1 Corinthians 3:2

13. Hebrews 5:12-14: 1 Corinthians 13:9-12. . John 13:33.

14. Galatians 6:7

15. I Corinthians 15:41

16. Luke 16:19-24.

17. Matthew 25;31-46.

18. See the appendix

19. Daniel 3:4-7

20. Revelations 4 chapter.

21.Matthew 26:51-52.

22. A Cours8. John 3:16;   2 John 4:8 Almost any chapter of the Koran   e In Miracles Published by The Foundation for Inner Peace.

23. The Nature of personal Reality Bantam Books by Jane Roberts

24.   I Samuel 28: 6-20;Isaiah 6:1-4; Revelations 1:10-18; and First Samuel 28: 3-19.

25. Isaiah 28:7-13 and 1 Corinthians 13:9-12.

26. Genesis 2:15

27. Air pollution and pollution in the north and in big cities.

28.Genesis 1:28

29. Most "Holy Books" teach respect for the Earth.

For more information see appendix #2

16:   Principles For living in Peace

There is a basic and fundamental reality that we need to point out as we enter into this discussion. This is the truth that what we do to others we do to ourselves. This is the basis of the "Golden Rule" 1 Jesus also pointed this out when he said "In the same way you judge others, you will be judged and with the measure you use, it will be measured to you." 2.

The fact is that the time lag time between the handing out and the getting back varies greatly. Adolf Hitlers' "Third Reich" that he boasted would last a thousand years was in ashes within about fifteen years at the cost of fifty million lives and most of the leaders were dead or on trial. The Jews organized the crucifixion of Jesus and it took about forty years for that to come back to them. The adage "what comes around goes around" says it well. In some cases it may not come back in this lifetime but only at the "Eternal Judgement" referred to in the last part of this chapter.

Keeping this in mind no-one has the right to impose, or try to impose their ideas on another. People must all learn to RESPECT and honour other folks rights to freedom of choice.

Hope is fundamental to life. Without hope people shrivel up and some commit suicide. Farmers who depend on the weather must have

147

hope. In some circles the farmers say "it is a next year country" because they hope for better next year. Business men who risk resources on a project must have hope. If we have no hope we will not try and nothing can improve in out lives unless we take the responsibility to have hope and act on it. People who have no hope will put illegal mind altering agents into their bodies. They will do many destructive things driven by their fears and desperation. They will not have respect for themselves or others. They will also deny the truth of this statement thinking, foolishly, that denial is a refuge. Lack of hope in eternal life, a life of joy, drives people to desperate measures. Somehow we need to instil hope in our youth. They need to understand that all things are possible if they have the desire, respect for others and faith.

Love   is the lubricant that greases the wheels of life. God is love and God as parent wants the best for "Its" children, wants the best for each of us. It is evidenced in our world, given to us and which is   capable of meeting all our needs. However love is not to be confused with slackness or weakness. Strong love does not enable drug addicts to continue their path to self destruction. It does not sweep murder under the rug and it does not condone misuse of power. Wise and loving parents do not allow children to do as they please.

They discipline and train them as needed and they do not abandon them to fate. They are also always there for their children. Can God do any less for IT's children? God's love is demonstrated for us in the fact that we have a wonderful home: Mother Earth. Everything is recycled and so the life expectancy for Earth is long enough that we need not worry. Our worry is that we might destroy our home by bickering and fighting. Or we could be in the way when Earth goes through one of her cataclysmic disturbances. (It is to be noted here that such a cataclysm is not necessarily a judgement of God against anyone) If we are killed in one such upheaval, we have to count on Gods' love and the promise of life beyond the grave. That is Gods final promise that we will not be deserted.

<u>Freedom</u>; is ours whether by Gods design or otherwise. It comes with a price. That price is the consequence attached to every choice that we make. We are compelled to make choices every day. Even choosing to NOT make a choice IS a choice. Because it is Gods' gift to us it cannot be taken from anyone, except with their complicity. Even in chains the human mind is free. We are free to choose but each choice carries a consequence. That is the price of freedom. Freedom gives each of us a free mind that only we can imprison and that only by choice. It places a great deal of

149

responsibility on each one of us to exercise our freedom with care and good judgement. Freedom may be illustrated by the old saw; "convince a person against their will and they will be of the same opinion still." People have been put in chains, burned at the stake and other wise abused and yet retained their freedom of thought. Only if one believes in the everlasting nature of their consciousness and the appropriateness of their cause can one freely choose to defy such a death threat. Their choice must also recognize and honor the freedom of others.

Accountability

The principle is that what you put out returns to you. Therefore you are accountable whether you like it or not. If my life is not the way I want it blaming someone else does not fix it. My choices brought me to this undesirable place. Only by my choices and action can the place be changed to a more acceptable state. Sure I may be able to enlist the help of a friend, or God or whom ever but it is always my choice and it is my responsibility to make the request. That request flows from repentance. If not to make the request, at least to accept the offered aid and to accept the responsibility for my choice. In simple form this is easy to see. I may choose to touch the stove to see if it is hot. It may burn my finger. Might I not have

150

found a safer way to do the test? However I chose and I paid with a burned finger. When my choices involve the assistance of others it is easy to pass blame and not realize that I chose those others and now may resent them if things do not work out as I planned.

Faith, We are told that without faith it is impossible to please God. However, without faith it is impossible to live. We choose to act in faith every day, when we venture out on the streets, when we eat food someone else has prepared and in a myriad of ways. We do these acts of faith most often in automatic mode. We do not think of them as acts of faith. We take these actions for granted. These acts are listed in chapter nine. Perhaps we need to develop our faith in people. No doubt we will have many disappointments in so doing but in the end we might be happier than we are now. People respond or re-act according to how they are treated in most cases. When you expect the best from someone you are more likely to get it than if you expect the worst. Just imagine how you would feel if someone came up to you and talked down in a very demanding tone. Would you give that person your best with love? If not how can you expect that Third World person to give you their best if you treat them in such a fashion? Is that not how we often treat a person that we consider of less importance than the average? We need to treat people equally. 3 Lack of faith in our fellow humans has not been productive of peace or

freedom for all. Would not these principles imply that freedom for all was the goal?

<u>Honesty</u> is a vital requirement. I must at least be honest with and to myself. Otherwise I am in denial and stuck where I am. Honesty is listed before repentance because I cannot repent if I deny my part in the situation. An honest appraisal of the situation allows me to consider alternatives. Honesty also is required before I can admit to another that I have been wrong or have harmed them in some way. There is an element of confession in true honesty. Without the recognition of confession no change can take place. Reconciliation is not a possibility until I can be honest with myself and someone I have offended. The same thing would apply when someone offends me.

<u>Repentance,</u> is simply the willingness to learn from mistakes and try a different way next time. Part of it is taking responsibility for ones own actions as nothing can change until each of us does just that. Once we take responsibility for our own actions only, then can changes be made. Remember that one definition of insanity is doing the same thing over and over expecting to get a

different result. Some times we might be required to say "I'm sorry" as part of our repentance.

Especially if someone is hurt by our actions.

Because we usually cannot see the end of the train of consequences that come with our choices, we are likely to hurt people inadvertently. Is harm done in ignorance as hurtful as when it is done deliberately? Even if the harm is the same might not your heart be softened a little when you know it was not intended? Saying "I'm sorry" is not enough. We must also show by our actions that we mean it. Learning from our mistakes is one definition of repentance as I see it. Might it be possible that no one has all the answers and so repentance and teachability might be good for all of us? May we all need to learn to listen more and talk (scream) less?

Forgiveness is fundamental to progress. We are bound to be hurt and to hurt people inadvertently if not by design. Carrying grudges for hundred and thousands of years and demanding restitution or reparation from people who were not responsible or even born is disastrous. One of the most important people to forgive is self. It is not practical to move ahead into the light while I drag my fear, remorse and guilt along. I must learn to take the lesson and leave the guilt. Repentance is of no value if I cannot or will not forgive. Jesus

tells us that if we do not forgive neither will God. 4
The big question might be who will make the
first move? Because our self worth is often
attached to being right and losing face might seem
wrong, people often hold back. Keeping up
appearances is based on pride and haughtiness.
Honesty and repentance cannot work where that
kind of pride is at work. Further, what if your
overture was rejected? Might it be possible that
God would see that you had done your part even if
your overture was rejected? I think that if your
conscience is now clear God will be O. K. with
you. Remember that you can only control yourself.
You cannot control what others may or may not do
in response to your action.

<u>Immersion</u> in the project is also vital. In church
it is usually called baptism however it has far more
wide reaching significance. It may be the symbol
of our accepting Divine Grace and forgiveness.
The symbol of the forgiveness for mistakes. There
is very often an argument about the method of
baptism. Should it be by immersion or by
sprinkling? Some say that baptism is a necessity
and must be done correctly to count. These would
argue that it must be in water and by immersion.
Others would agree that immersion is important
but immersion in the work might be more to the
point than immersion in the water. Would this not

be true especially if the commitment went no further than the water? People may be immersed in peace making, religion or any one of dozens of projects. In one sense might your immersion in this project be your acceptance of the values and the affirmation of your interest in practicing the preceding principles? Many people are already immersed in this work and process. Many others totally disregard all of these principles and are immersed in contrary goals and processes. Might not the world be changed for the better in a very short time if these values were held; and practiced, by all? Of course a person could become immersed in terrorism instead. However terrorism does not comply with the above principles as it does not support life. We must always think carefully about our choices and what we invest ourselves in. The consequences may have eternal significance.

<u>Confirmation</u> might be the seal of Divine approval on those who embrace choices and actions that are kind to Earth and are life supporting. Most churches go through a process whereby their members are "confirmed" into the church. However only God can truly confirm. That confirmation will be an inner knowing and possibly a sense of empowerment when one is engaged in the work that God approves of. <u>5</u> Sadly

this may exclude some church authorities from the experience. An example might be the authorities who condemned Galileo and Copernicus for daring to suggest that the earth was not flat. Confirmation may be misleading when one gets confirmation from a superior for actions considered unacceptable to God. An example would be the confirmation given to the operators of the "Death Camps" by their superiors during WW 2 or the acts of terrorists. Humanity is revolted by such actions. We might ask "where was their conscience?" It is possible to train ones conscience to accept and approve of terrible acts, especially when we are ordered by our authorities. Conscience is not always a safe guide. We need to invest careful thought as well. Only God can confirm and so few get the confirmation that many abdicate their personal responsibility and allow the others to make up rules to satisfy themselves. However perhaps we should be thinking about applying these principles to our own lives. Would not our lives be easier and more productive all around if we applied them to our everyday relationships? We could confirm our faith in others by actions if we chose to do so.

<u>Resurrection</u> is a principle that we see demonstrated in some form every day. It suggests the possibility of new life. We see it every spring.

We see it in the lives of persons released from the bondage of addiction and in renewed health for those recovering from major surgery. It may also be the promise of life beyond the grave. If human kind took the trouble to practice these principles, might we not see new life and hope for "Space Ship Earth" in the here and now? After all we do not know what happens in the hereafter but we certainly can influence what happens here. Our correctional systems, while far from perfect, do attempt to rehabilitate offenders. Our hospitals contain rehabilitation wings in an effort to give people new life. You see we practice resurrection almost daily in our lives. However, practicing it in unawareness may not be good enough. We need to practice life renewing actions deliberately and always. Life is eternal or endless. Might we all have the chance to experience new life here and now if these principles were the guiding stars of our lives?

Eternal Judgement shows up in the consequence that are experienced from the choices that we make as individuals and as a race. Judgement need not be hurtful or disastrous. Positive choices may well result in happy consequences. All the judgements we receive are not sad ones. We live with the consequences, and the judgements of our choices, every day of our lives. We choose the consequences when we choose the actions. This even if the train of consequences is so long that we cannot see all the coaches that are connected to it. This is the law of life. Do you think that the victims of the Tsunami that hit the Indian Ocean in 2004 expected that result when they made their homes along the shore? Or do you think that it was a judgement of God against them personally? Jesus did not seem to think that natural disasters or freak accidents were evidence of Gods' anger. 6

The eastern concept of karma has real significance in daily life. "Space Ship" Earth is experiencing judgement even now? Judgement also offers hope to human kind.

I now recognize the unity of all things. I see God is in all and that I am one with the ALL. I realize that I have a part to play in the bigger picture. I see that the above principles are of significant value in the process of peace making and consciousness raising on our Space Ship Earth. I can see how anger, bitterness and the desire for revenge has clouded our vision and is a path that inevitably leads to destruction. I can see the need for faith in myself and my fellow humans and the personal risk that that involves.

I deny the power of fear, anger and frustration to

block my path to enlightenment. The common notion that God is a mystery and cannot be known blocks the possibility of enlightenment. I deny its power to block me from enlightenment now.

I can see how these principles, properly practiced can open the way to awareness. New life is mine for the claiming and so I do the work.

I am one with "All That Is" and I see how what I do to others I do to myself.

Therefore I now claim my right and the right of all people to awareness and enlightenment. I am open to learn to see and to hear whatever light and truth The Divine has in store for me. I move forward in hope and joy as I claim my place and now release this treatment to the Infinite, knowing that it is so now. AND SO IT IS!

1. Matthew 7:12.
2. Matthew 7:2.
3. James 2:1-7.
4. Matthew 6:4.
5. Acts 2:1-4.
6. Matthew 6:14-15.
7. Luke 13:1-5.

Seventeen: My experience

I am now 76 years of age. The beliefs that I hold
and have advocated in this book are hard won.

Here, at least in part, is my story.

We lived on a farm. I was born in 1929, just before
the "great depression." My Dad had to cope with
drought and illness in the family. My Mother
made her transition when I was 10, just a few days
after WW 2 broke out. Thus Dad was left with
myself and a younger brother, a pile of debt and
failing health. However he always clung fast to his
faith in God. He said that farmers had to have faith
to make the investment of seed etc. in hopes of a
crop which did not always materialize.

Dad always taught us to think for ourselves. He
held a few fairly radical ideas. However his faith
never wavered and his endless concern for his two
boys was and still is a marker in my life.

One of the things Dad did was to make sure we
had a family worship each night. During these
times he read the scriptures to us and we talked. I
was sure that I was in the "right" church and that
God would protect me from all harm.

When I grew up I married a beautiful young
woman. (We later parted ways) When our first
child was due she could not deliver. The doctor did
a "C" section and all was well. Dan was a fine
strong boy. When our second son, David, was

born, again by "C" section he was hydrocephalic. The doctor said the best thing to happen for us was if we were not able to take him home. (In those days there was no treatment for hydrocephalic babies.)

So much for Gods' protection. I was very angry with God and terribly disappointed that things did not work out to my satisfaction. Or perhaps my religion was wrong and God was punishing me (us). I buried our son while my wife was still in hospital recovering from her second "C" section. Later driving my tractor in the field I cried and told God I was finished. "I don't need this church or you anymore."

At that very moment I heard the "still small voice" from within ask very casually "where will you go?" I was stumped. I could not answer the question. As I thought about this I noticed that the sun was shining, the crop was growing and the world went on. Even my tractor was running well. It was at this point that I had my first inkling of the truth that the world did not turn around me. (It was many years later when I learned how to explain what I call "basic sin.")

With no place to go I decided to stay where I was. In due course I left the farm for the big city. (This big city was less than half a million but it looked big to the farm boy.) Here a third son, Ray was born. Ray was an "RH" baby and had to have his blood changed immediately after his birth. This is probably why David did not live more than two days.

When the city doctor told me we would have an "RH" baby I said "this only happens to kings, it can't happen to us." However it did. Ray was pretty sick for a while and was in an incubator. I called for the ministers of the church to come and pray for him. My understanding was that they must touch the candidate. 1 However the minister who came said "if I cannot touch him we can proceed anyway." I objected but the nurse said "no problem" so he reached into the hand hole in the incubator and touched Ray as he prayed for him. I was so caught up in legalism where God was concerned that it was as if I thought God could not act without "the law" being fulfilled in all points. It did not occur to me to wonder how God got stuff done before there were elders.

Shortly after this happened I was called into ministry. In our church the ministers are self supporting, generally speaking. I was surprised and thought to refuse. However with wise counsel from about the third leader I counselled with, I decided to accept.

Some time after this I was asked to preach my first sermon. How I prepared! I "pounded" the Bible relentlessly. I also noticed that much of what I first thought to say conflicted with what I read. I worked on it for at least three months. It was a learning experience. I could choose my own leader for the service and I chose the minister who had come to pray for Fred. I told him to have a sermon in his pocket as I would likely freeze up. I was sacred out of my wits. His reply was terse and seemingly un-caring. He said "you should know better that to look to me for help." Of course he was saying "look to God" but at that moment I felt very alone.

When I stood up to read the lesson, I thought," they will not be able to find fault with this anyway. It is the words of Jesus." (I did not yet realize the possibility that the book of Matthew was written long after Jesus was gone.) In any event the experience was one I will never forget. I was focused and on track. I did not hear children cry or people cough. I was in my own world. Some congratulated me after the fact.

I "peddled milk" for the first years in the city. Not wanting to make a career of this, I found a job several years later in retail sales. In due course I was able to persuade my superiors that I should become manager. Shortly after this I was beaten up by a subordinate who did not like my policy. When all the dust settled I was given the choice of

163

A transfer or leaving the job. The "P. R. was bad," I was told.

I found a new job after a couple of weeks. (The only unemployment insurance I ever drew.)

This new job was with the government and took me out of town for long periods to work in a gaol (jail). I was able, after a couple of years to get transferred to a different department of government. The new placement was in Public Works. I had to write a mechanical aptitude test.

It was easy for a farm boy.

This job took me to the boiler room of a large heating and power generating plant. Here I was completely lost and my classification was "trainee." The first rule for trainees was "do not touch anything with out permission or supervision." This suited me because I had very little self confidence and no knowledge of the system.

In this job I found the noise and heat very disturbing. I thought I might have to quit. However as time passed I became acclimatized and began to feel O. K. I did the work and the studying required and soon got promoted to assistant engineer. I had the opportunity to gain experience in two other plants. It was interesting to note the fuss people in these other smaller plants made about responsibility. The Chief Engineer in the one I was trained in used to laugh at himself and say "I am just a stupid engineer but sometimes I must have your attention and obedience." The others in the much smaller plants where I spent some time seemed to carry the weight of the world on their shoulders. This was most true for the smallest plant I worked in.

In due course I got back to the big plant, did the studying required and eventually was advised that I would be promoted to replace the "Shift Engineer" who was leaving. "Are you sure?" I asked my boss. (my self confidence was still very low.) "Yes" he replied. I had always needed permission as an assistant engineer. Now it was my job to give permission. However I avoided this responsibility for a month or so by getting my permission from other authority figures available to me. Some of them complained about this. Came the day when a rather unusual request came to me from the people in charge of servicing the buildings. No authority figures were to be found. I came to realize that it was my job and I had to give permission. (I think a bit of spiritual insight was given to me that day.)

Years later I took the shift one evening and found a note from the Chief Engineer asking me to make sure the new boiler was loaded by morning as it was to be put through its' paces by the builder the next day.

Well into the shift, my assistant came to me and reported that he had heard a strange noise. He could not place it and as I had instructed, "anything you do not understand should be reported to me." We inspected the plant and found nothing. A couple of hours later he came again with the same story. I wanted to pooh, pooh the whole thing but my "inner voice," said "listen to him." I got a scolding from that inner voice and was told to "do my job."

This boiler was the biggest in our line up. I walked around the plant trying to figure out what the fuss was. I ended up standing in the noisiest place in the plant. I noticed that the fan louvers were flapping, not good! I walked around the fan and saw bolts missing, which my assistant had heard as they hit the fan. Of course there was no follow up sound of an unusual nature till the next bolt came out. The control system on the fan was failing. This fan was driven by a four hundred and fifty horse power motor and was feeding air to a boiler operating at 900 pounds per square inch of steam pressure with a temperature of 800 degrees F. It was also burning about four hundred thousand cubic feet of natural gas per hour at that moment. I wasted no time in ordering it shut down. When my people objected "the orders were to load it" I said "just do what you are told." Probably several lives were saved as well as property by this shut down.

"Somebody (God?) was looking after me and us too. Our plant was sitting beside a major hospital. When the big parts of the control system got into the fan who knows what would happen.

Earlier in my experience a Regional Supervisor (one of the few professionals in our church) came to our church for a business meeting. He was to speak at the worship service and it fell to me to lead. As he spoke I became impressed that God wanted to say something to this man. I though "how nice and exciting." As he went on I began to wonder who would God choose to be the spokesman. As I looked over the congregation and saw the leaders, I was reminded that God operates in an orderly fashion. 2 My understanding was that God recognized authority and as the leader I was in authority for that moment. I began to realize that I was to be the spokesman. I was scared out of my wits again, (something I seemed to be able to experience quite often.)

In any event I did stand up when he was finished. I had the sense of what was needed but God gave me no words. These I had to find for myself. I told him God was pleased with his efforts. Later I found out that he had experienced a nervous break down and our region was his first assignment since his recovery. I think he needed reassurance and perhaps even permission to go on. After the service some people thanked me for speaking up.

Another experience I had was in a service where people were invited to share. As the service was drawing to a close, the leader asked if there were any more testimonies. No one spoke but I said "I would like to comment" and he said "go ahead." I addressed my remarks to two ladies in the group. Both had been through tough times lately. I tried to find the words to express my sense of what God wanted them to know. Words of Divine comfort love and approval. When I sat down the leader opinioned that the message was valid and came from God, as did some other people later.

I took early retirement from the heating plant. My new problem was what to do with my time. Among other things I took two units of "Clinical Pastoral Education in a major hospital. I also took a course in "Life Skills Coach Training." Here they spent a lot of time talking about feelings. I had shut my feelings off many years before. I was sceptical about the whole thing and could not ever find the "right" answer to any issue that came up. I think I felt above these folks and I wondered about the leaders. Far into the course a young lady excitedly reported a tingling and other feelings that I do not remember. However the Trainer said to her "you are getting your innocence back." She had a technical explanation. However my thinking was "there is more here that I ever thought if this happens. Only God can do this." Up to this time I tended to think God operated only in church or even only in "our" church. To see God operating in a Life Skills group was an eye opener for me.

Later a year or so I was counselling with a family where the wife had been on the street for years before she married. I remember asking her at one point, "if I could see you as God sees you, what would I see?" Her answer was unhesitating. "Rot" she said. I think that God showed me how He saw her. I felt as if I had intruded into a sacred and private place. Everything was clean and spotless, bright and holy.

From this experience I learned to avoid making judgments about people. I do not know their life experience or pain. I am to take them as they are and share Gods' love with them. That is all.

From this back ground and from fairly extensive studies I came to the place where this book HAD to be written. It is written in the hope that it may at least shed a little bit of light into our dark world. We have so much strife in our world and only the realization that we are all one, that what we do to others we do also to ourselves can open us to peace. God bless you all as you read and

169

understand.

I am convinced that there is one mind, one power and one source from which all things flow and to which all things return. Therefore each one of us is a small particle of that major source that I call God. This "God" expresses Its self in an infinite number of ways. Each of us is one such way. Concepts of "good and evil" do not apply. Both good and evil are concepts discerned in the eye of the beholder.

Whatever happens, the Universe or God absorbs and recycles all for the continued sustenance of a system so large that we cannot begin to conceive of it all. A system that is endless and eternal with neither beginning one end. Beginning and ending are only limiting human ideas.

I accept my place in this system with joy and faith. I am here to expand my knowledge and talents. I am ready for the next step in my endless journey. In the meantime I testify and advocate hope, love and brotherhood for all. I am one with "All That Is!" And So It Is!

1. James 5:13-15
2. 1 Corinthians 14:29-33.

Appendix "A"

The Blind Men and the Elephant

Twas six men of Indostan
To learning much inclined
Who went to see the elephant,
(Thought all of them were blind).
That each by observation
Might satisfy his mind.

The first approached the elephant,
And happening to fall
Against his broad and sturdy side,
At once began to bawl,
"God bless me but the elephant
Is very like a wall."

The second feeling the tusk,
Cries "Ho What have we here
So very round and smooth and sharp?
To me, tis mighty clear,
This wonder of an elephant
Is very like a spear."

The third approached the animal
and happening to take
The squirming trunk within his hands,

Thus boldly up did spake:
"I see" quoth he "the Elephant
Is very like a snake."

The fourth reached out an eager hand,
And felt about the knee.
"What most this wonderous beast is like
Is mighty plain" quoth he:
"Tis clear enough the Elephant
Is very like a tree."

The fifth who chanced to touch the ear,
Said "E'en the blindest man
Can tell, what this resembles most:
Deny the fact who can,
This marvel of an Elephant
Is very like a fan."

The sixth no sooner had begun
About the Elephant to grope,
Then siezing on the swinging tail
That fell within his scope.
"I see" quoth he, "The Elephant
 Is very like a rope."

And so these men of Indostan
Disputed loud and long,
Each in his own opinion

Exceeding stiff and strong,
Though each was partly right
And all of them were wrong.

Moral

So oft in theologic wars,   "---now I
The disputants, I ween   know in part---."
Rail on in utter ignorance   Apostle Paul
 Of what each other mean,   1 Corinthians
And prate about the Elephant   13:11-12.
Not one of them has seen.

By the American Poet
John Godfrey Saxe.

Appendix "B"

A few passages from the Bhagavad-Gita and the King James bible compared.

(The Bhagavad-Gita is a major book of Hindu scripture.) Translated by A. C. Bhaktivedanta Swami Prabhupada

Bhagavad-Gita	King James Bible
In His different incarnations Lord Krsna assumes three Visnus---Maha-Visnu, creator of material Energy--the second --creates Diversity --third is diffused as as all pervading.	"--I Am Alpha and Omega the beginning and the end. Rev. 21:4-6. God the Father

173
.

Purport on 7:4
P.124.

(Creator) the beginning
Jesus Son and Holy
Spirit, all pervading.

"He who knows me as unborn,
as the beginningless, as the
Supreme Lord of all the worlds
--he, undeluded among men, is
freed from all sins."
10:3

"I am that I am"
Exodus 3:13-14.
"I am The Lord."
Leviticus 11"44-5.
In these God is
revealing but not
known.

"I am the source of everything:"
from Me the entire creation
flows. Knowing this,
the wise worship
Me with all their. hearts."
10:8

"--I am He, and there is
no God with me" "I
kill and I makealive,
none can deliver
out of my hand."
Deuteronomy 32:39.

"Never was there a time I
did not exist," nor you, nor
all these kings; nor in the
future shall any of us cease
to be."
2: 12."

"The eternal God is
thy refuge, and
underneath are the ever-.
lasting arms."
Deuteronomy 33:27.
"I am Alpha and Omega,
the beginning and the end,
The first and the last."
Revalation 22:13.

"As a man leaves an old garment
and puts on one that is new, the
spirit leaves his mortal body and
then puts on one that is new."
2:22

"For we know that if our
earthly house of this
tabernacle were
dissolved we have a
building of God,
an house not made

174

"That which pervades the
entire body is indestructible--
the imperishable soul."
2:17.
"Man can find peace in the
peace of God." 2:72

"A faithful man who is absorbed
in trancendetal knowledge and
who subdues his senses, quickly
attains the supreme spiritual
peace." 4:39.
"But it is I who am the ritual,
I the sacrifice, the offering to
the ancestors, the healing
herb, the transcendental chant;
I am the butter and the fire
and the offering."
9:16.
"Know that all beautiful, glorious,
mighty creations spring from
but a spark of My splendor."
10:41

with hands, --."
2 Corinthians 5:1

"Peace I leave with you,
my peace give unto you-
--." John 14:27.

"--the truth shall make
you free."
John 8:32.
"---my peace I give to
you--." John 14:27.
"---but now once in the
end of the world hath he
appeared to put away sin
by the sacrifice of
himself."
Heb. 9:26.

Finally, brethern,
whatsoever things are
true, whatsoever
things are honestt,
whatsoever things are
just, whatsoever things
are pure, whatsoever
things are lovely,
whatsoever things
are of good report;
if there be any virtue,
and if there be any praise,
think on these things."
Phillipians 4:8

175

"Only in love can men see me and come unto me." 11:54

"A new commandment I give unto you that you love one another as I have loved you, that ye also love one another John 13:34.

"One who is equal to friends and enemies, who is equipoised in honour and dishonour, heat and cold, happiness and distress, fame and infamy, who is always free from contamination,always silent, and satisfied with anything, who doesn't care for any residence, who is fixed in knowledge and engaged in devotional service, is very dear to me."
12:18-19.

"Ye have heard --but I say unto you, Love your enemies, bless them that curse you --and pray for them which despitefully use you and persecute you ----for (God) makes His sun to rise on the evil and on good, and sends rain on the just and the unjust."
Matthew 5:43-46

"I am the father, mother, and grandfather of all this universe, I am what is known, I am purity----, I am the goal, the upholder, the master, the witness, the home, the shelter and most dear friend. I am the creation and the annihilation the basis of everything, the resting place and the eternal seed."
." 9:17-18.

"--I, am He and there is no God with me: I kill, and I make alive; I wound, and I heal: neither is there any that can deliver out of my hand."
Deut. 32:39.
"I am the Lord, and there is none else. I form the light, and create darkness: I make peace and create evil: I the Lord do all these

The Koran and the Bible

things."   Isaiah 45:6-7.

In the name of (Allah) the
Compassionate, the merciful

Say "O ye unbelievers!
I worship not that which
ye worship, And ye do
Not worship that which I
worship;   I shall never
worship that which ye
worship. Niether will
ye worship that which
I worship. To you be
your religion; to me
be my religion."
 Sura CIX UNBELIEVERS

"He that is unjust, let him
 be unjust still: and he which

 Is filthy, let him be filthy
 still----."
Revelations 22:11.

"Judge not, that ye be not
judged. For with what
judgement ye judge,
ye shall be judged: and
with what measure ye
mete, it shall be measured
to you again."
Mat. 7:1-2

Remember when God (Allah)
Said "O Jesus! verily I will
cause thee to die, and will
take thee up to myself and
deliver thee from those who
believe not, until the Day of
Resurrection. Then, to Me is
your return, and wherein ye
differ will I decide between
you."   Sura III:48.

"God so loved the
world, that He gave
His only begotten Son,
that whosoever believeth
in him should not perish
 but have everlasting life."
 John 3:16.

And when the sacred months
are past, kill those who join

See the entire 20 chapter
of Deuteronomy.

177

other gods with God (Allah)
Wherever ye shall find them;
and seize them and besiege
them, and lay wait for them
with every kind of ambush:
but if they shall convert--let
them go, for God (Allah) is

"leave nothing alive in
the cities of the land
The Lord your God is
giving you."
V 16.

merciful."
Sura IX:5

A thief, whether man or woman
should have their hands cut
off in recompense for
their doings.
Sura V:42.

A man gathering wood
on the Sabbath is to be
stoned to death.
Numbers 15:32-36

.

"In the Name of God (Allah?),
the Compassionate, the
Merciful
What thinkest thou of him
who treateth our RELIGEON
as a lie? He it is who thrusteh
away the orphan, And
stirreth not others up to
feed the poor. Woe to those
who pray, But in their prayer
Are careless; Who make
a shew of devotion, But
refuse help to the needy."
Sura CVII

"Therefore all things
whatsoever ye would
that men should do to
you, do ye even so to
to them: for this is the
law and the prophets."
Matthew 7:12.

"Not every one who
says unto me , Lord, ,
Lord, shall enter into
the kingdom of
heaven; but he that
doeth the will of my
Father which is in
heaven."
Matthew 7:21.

178

ISBN 141208801-1

This work challenges the thinker in us all. It examines the foundations of faith, the concepts of God, and questions the validity of some of the long held beliefs about how God might or might not deal with people all over the face of the earth. It asks the reader to update their religion rather than keep focused on heroes of the past; many of whom thought that the world was flat. Such people might not have a sense, or need a sense, of the "Universal God of all." Morris Johnstone suggests that changing concepts of time and space require updated concepts of God.

It is food for thought and written by a deep thinker. Each chapter ends with an affirmative prayer designed so that the reader may easily make it personal to themselves.

Interesting!

ISBN 141208801-1

9 781412 088015

TRAFFORD
PUBLISHING™